After The Gold Rush

Growing Up In Skagway

Robert A. Dahl

Copyright © 2005 by Robert A. Dahl.

Library of Congress Number:		2005900388
ISBN:	Hardcover	1-4134-8411-5
	Softcover	1-4134-8410-7

All rights reserved. No part of this book may be reproduced or transmitted in any form or by any means, electronic or mechanical, including photocopying, recording, or by any information storage and retrieval system, without permission in writing from the copyright owner.

This book was printed in the United States of America.

To order additional copies of this book, contact:
Xlibris Corporation
1-888-795-4274
www.Xlibris.com
Orders@Xlibris.com

26771

Contents

Chapter	Page
Acknowledgement	vi
1. We Arrive	1
2. Skagway: the Gold Rush Town	4
3. Why We Moved to Skagway	11
4. Pansies in Winter	19
5. The Town	25
6. Who Were They?	31
7. The Midnight Sun, 1930	40
8. A Walk Up Broadway	49
9. The Midnight Sun, 1934	61
10. Off Broadway	75
11. The Midnight Sun, 1935	81
12. At School	90
13. At Work: on the Dock	97
14. At Work: the Railroad Section	105
15. At Play	113
16. A Journey to Goatland	118
17. The Grizzly	129
18. The Best Years of Their Lives	137
19. Town Characters: Comedy, Pathos . . .	146
20 . . . . And Tragedy	154
21. Outcasts in Their Own Land	162
22. We Leave	172
About the Author	183

Photographs

Picture	Page
Skagway from the Sea	2
Dyea Wharf, Circa 1897	5
Chilkoot Pass, Winter of 1898	6
White Pass, Winter of 1899	7
Harriet Pullen	8
Soapy Smith in His Saloon	9
The Tropea House	21
The Town of Skagway	26
Broadway	50
The Hospital	59
The Rapuzzi House	78
An Evening on the Front Porch	79
The School	90
White Pass Railroad train 17 Miles from Skagway	105
Heading up the Tracks	107
Lunch in the Sun	111
The Basketball Team	114
Dreaming of Glory, Age 10 or 11	118
Lew with a Goat	125
Myself with a Goat	125
A Full Pack	126
Lew with the Bear	134
Myself with the Bear	134
The Mighty Hunters	135

Photographs, Continued

Picture	Page
Mother and Dad	138
Martin Itjen	147
Glacier Bay around 1933	158
Margery Glacier	158
Tlingit Carved Wood Figures	162
Three brothers, headmen of the Chilkat Tlingit, Alaska, 1907	163
Best Wishes from Skagway	176
Skagway, the Lynn Canal, and the Mountains Beyond	181

Acknowledgements

As we all know, memories can be tricky and self-serving. And as trial lawyers well know, one person's recollections, even if honest and well intended, may not match those of another who was present at the same event. I imagine that the five hundred people living in Skagway in the twenties and thirties might have remembered those years in five hundred different ways.

To buttress my own no doubt faulty memory in writing this memoir, I've been enormously helped by Carl Nord's collection of biographies of people who have lived in Skagway from 1897 onward.

My brother Roger, who was just three when we arrived in Skagway, lived there longer than I did, and perhaps remembered aspects of it better. To jog my memory as I've covered some of the same ground, I've drawn freely on his "My Life in Skagway," which he wrote in 1989. Thanks, Roger, and thanks, too, for reading an early draft of my manuscript and offering some corrections and suggestions.

For the early history of Skagway and Dyea, Pierre Berton's *The Klondike Fever* (New York, 1958) was a marvelously entertaining and, I believe, highly reliable source. In preparation for that book, Berton interviews many of the still surviving pioneers of the Klondike gold-rush.

In addition to Berton, I've drawn on several other published works, which are cited in the memoir.

I've also made use of *The Midnight Sun* which was "edited and published," as the masthead announced with some grandiosity, by Lewis Dahl, Rodney Johnston, and Robert Dahl during the summer of 1930, by Lewis and Robert Dahl the summer of 1934, and by me the summer of 1935.

Finally, I've drawn on the transcript I'd had made of Mother's recollections taped on her 90th birthday, October 17, 1979. Though Roger, Irene, Marilyn, Kit, and I all intervened occasionally, it was Ann's skilful probing that produced most of the information.

I am indebted to Tom Casey, who on a visit to Skagway secured useful information and photos for me. With his premature death I have lost a valued friend, as have his fellow graduate students, everyone who knew him, and Alaska.

Through Tom Casey and by e-mail, Judith Munns, director of the Skagway Museum, gave me access to the resources of the Museum. Carl Mulvihill offered several helpful comments on the first version.

Barbara Dedman, who was born in Skagway and is a unique source of memories about the town, not only corrected several factual errors in the book as it first appeared, but, as readers will see, she also drew on the extraordinary body of photos at the Dedman Photo Shop to provide a number of those that now appear in the book. Scott Mulvihill was kind enough to provide the beautiful photograph on the last page.

Lastly, I want to express my thanks to two persons who made crucial contributions to the final form of this memoir. As she has with my other writings over the past three decades, Ann, with her keen editorial eye, read every chapter and offered suggestions and corrections that improved the style and content of the final version. To make the memoir more widely available than the few copies that I would have produced myself for family members, in the midst of his busy schedule Eric volunteered to take on the task of editing and formatting the book that is now before you. His superb and highly professional editing of the final manuscript eliminated many typographical and stylistic errors and omissions.

North Haven, Connecticut
December 2, 2002

After the Gold Rush
Growing up in Skagway

1. We Arrive

As the darkness of a January morning begins to give way to daylight, the ship rounds the last point on our route, and there, directly ahead, lies Skagway.

Lew and I were too excited to sleep long this morning and we awoke early. After gulping down our breakfast, we made our way impatiently toward the bow. Roger soon joins us. Mother is in her stateroom still, no doubt busy with last minute packing.

It is January 15, 1926. Roger is three years old, Lew is eleven, and I'm ten. Not long ago, back in Iowa, we celebrated our three December birthdays—Lew's on the 11th, mine on the 17th, and Roger's on Christmas day. Of those birthdays and Christmas I now remember nothing, though I think that despite Mother's brave efforts they must have been a bit forlorn because we missed Dad, who had left for Skagway early in December.

We can now see the town. It lies in a narrow valley that appears to be slightly above sea level and all but surrounded by snow-covered, fjord-like mountains that rise up steeply from the sea. On the western side of the valley a river rushes down to the sea. On the eastern mountain we make out a waterfall cascading down the snowy slope. Beyond the town to the north, the mountains appear to join. As we will learn, however, the White Pass—the famous Trail of '98—threads its narrow way between these mountains, and over it runs a narrow gauge railroad bearing the impressive name of the White Pass and Yukon Route Railroad. The White Pass, as we will soon learn to call it, has, you might say, brought us to Skagway.

By moving from Inwood, Iowa, to Skagway, Alaska, we have changed our surroundings in ways that on the morning of our arrival are still mainly unknown to us, but obviously they are extraordinary. Back in Inwood the highest hills a few miles from the town rose hardly two hundred feet above the endless plains. We could barely imagine how sea and mountains might look. Now we are surrounded by them.

We Arrive

During the last day or so of our three-day rail trip from Iowa to Seattle we saw our first mountains, and even now, all these years later, I can still recall the exhilaration I felt on waking up in Montana to a view of the Rocky Mountains, which I hardly knew existed. Later, during the five days we spent on the Canadian Pacific ship Princess Mary, traveling the thousand miles from Seattle to Skagway, we passed through the narrow fjords of Southern Alaska and saw towns huddled, like Skagway, between sea and mountain—Ketchikan, Sitka, Juneau, Wrangell. Yet the fjords, mountains, glaciers, rivers, waterfalls, mile after mile of mysterious and seemingly impenetrable dense green forests, and the sea, that long arm of the Pacific buttressed on the east by steep mountains and on the west by huge islands that sometimes opened to the great Pacific ocean beyond—all this was still wholly unfamiliar, overwhelming in its beauty and mystery, fascinating, a bit threatening, and yet powerfully attractive and inviting.

And now at last, growing closer and more visible by the minute, is our new home. Skagway.

Skagway from the Sea

What will it be like, living in this town of Skagway? Will the kids be friendly? Or will they treat us like ignorant outsiders from Iowa, which, I have to admit, we really are? Will our teachers be as nice as the ones we had back in Inwood? When the Skagway kids aren't in school, I wonder, what do they do with themselves? Do they perhaps climb those awesome and probably dangerous mountains I see rising all around? Can boys like us from the prairies, like Lew and I, ever learn to do scary things like that?

The long wooden dock that runs out from the town along the steep edge of the mountain on the east is rapidly coming into view. Which of us first spots Dad I no longer remember. But now see him on the dock. He is waving to us.

We're here.

2. Skagway: the Gold Rush Town

"The town of Skagway was conceived in lawlessness and nurtured in anarchy."

This is how Pierre Berton describes the place in his excellent account of the Klondike Gold Rush.[1]

Of the half dozen routes by which gold seekers attempted to reach the Yukon River and the Klondike, probably the two most heavily used were the Chilkoot Pass out of Dyea and the White Pass out of Skagway. (In Skagway, later, we called them the Trail of '97 and the Trail of '98.)

Dyea and Skagway both lie on valley floors at the end of Lynn Canal,[2] the northern extremity of the Inside Passage. The two valleys are only about three miles apart, separated by a low rise that forms the long foot of AB Mountain[3], and by the two rivers that run adjacent to the mountain. As I've already mentioned, the Skagway River abuts the eastern (or Skagway) side of AB; the more formidable Dyea River runs along the other side of the mountain.

Although it would have been easy for those driven by their hunger for Klondike gold to walk over that low foot of AB Mountain, the rivers were formidable obstacles, particularly on the Dyea side. As a result, for decades the only feasible way between the two towns was by boat.

---

[1] *The Klondike Fever* (New York, 1958): 149. In what follows I have drawn extensively from Berton, Ch. 4, 146-170, and Ch. 10, 333-365.

[2] Which is not a canal in the usual sense but rather a natural channel hemmed in by mountains that forms the final stretch of the Inside Passage.

[3] So named because a set of shallow canyons form the letters A and B joined at the spine. They are particularly visible in late spring and early summer when the snow has melted off the rest of the mountain leaving only the white snow in the canyons.

When we lived in Skagway, Dyea was a ghost town with a few decaying buildings scattered here and there. (I believe it remains so today.) Its population, as I remember, consisted of one hermit, one horse (presumably the property of the hermit) and, when the salmon were running in the river, a fair number of grizzly bears gorging themselves on the fish.

In flood stage from melting snows, the Dyea River would sometimes cut into the low bank that bounded the western edge of the town. Erosion might then cause a shack left over from the Gold Rush to tumble into the river and ride out into Lynn Canal, where we might see it from Skagway, floating around the bay like a weird, capsized boat until it finally broke up under the impact of the waves.

Dyea Wharf, Circa 1897

From the summer of 1897 through 1898, Dyea went from empty flats to a frenetic gold-rush settlement and then to a ghost town. During those two years thousands of gold-seekers poured into the town and thousands left it to struggle up the Chilkoot Pass. Those who managed to reach Lake Bennett some miles on the other side of the Pass, and were still driven onward by their desire for gold, built boats that they hoped, often mistakenly, would be good enough to carry them to the headwaters of the Yukon and then down that great river to the Klondike country.

For a seasoned climber the Chilkoot Pass would be a breeze. So it may be for the scores who, I'm told, now hike over it during the summer. But many of the gold seekers had little or no experience with the strenuous demands of crossing over a mountain. For the inexperienced newcomer (in Alaskan lingo the Cheechako), crossing over the Chilkoot Pass could be daunting, particularly in winter. Millions of people, I'd guess, have seen the famous photo of a line of heavily laden men and horses struggling through deep snows at an angle of 30-35 degrees where the trail rises abruptly from the base to the summit of the Pass.

Chilkoot Pass, Winter of 1898

Making the task even more arduous, no one was allowed to cross over into Canada without enough food to last him through a year—which meant something over a thousand pounds. That sensible rule was rigidly enforced by the Royal Canadian Mounted Police stationed just over the border. One winter trip over the pass was enough to discourage the less stouthearted Cheechako. Yet to bring in the required food plus other supplies necessary for his survival, the determined gold seeker might have to make as many as thirty trips.

The causes for the abrupt demise of the Chilkoot Pass as the preferred route to the interior, and therefore of Dyea as the town from which to start, lay only a few miles away: the White Pass and Skagway.

When we arrived in 1926, you could still see the remains of an abandoned and crumbling wharf running down the tide flats and out into the bay. We called it Moore's wharf, though most of us who lived in Skagway at that time hadn't the foggiest idea who Moore was. What we didn't know or appreciate was the fact that its builder had been one Captain William Moore, who had arrived in the late 1880s at the empty valley that would wield the deathblow to Dyea. For Moore's enduring contribution was not his wharf. It was his "discovery" of the White Pass and its advantages. It was Moore who crossed over and surveyed the twisting pass leading north out of Skagway, aided by Skookum Jim, the Indian co-discoverer with George Carmack of the nuggets that had set the whole Klondike gold rush in motion.[4] Bad as it was, the White Pass

---

[4] He gave it the name that it bore thereafter, not—as I had always thought—because it was deep in snow during the winter, but in honor of Sir Thomas White, the Canadian Minister of the Interior. Berton, p. 147.

out of Skagway was easier to traverse than the Chilkoot Pass. It rapidly became the preferred route— first by foot and then by rail. Construction of the White Pass & Yukon Railroad, connecting Skagway to Whitehorse, began in 1898 and was completed on July 29, 1900. Dyea became a ghost town. Skagway boomed.

White Pass, Winter of 1899

Like Dyea earlier, the narrow valley was soon crammed with several thousand men in pursuit of quick riches; with tents, shacks, ramshackle stores, a hotel or two, gambling dens and gamblers, bars and dancing girls, whorehouses and whores, con men, thugs . . . .

In a population that sometimes reached ten thousand, there were also a handful of women who had accompanied their husbands or perhaps were widows determined to achieve a better life for themselves and their children. "Even women entered the lucrative packing trade," Berton writes. Among them was Harriet Pullen, a widow with four sons, who arrived in September, 1897, "with seven dollars in her pocket and parlayed it into a comfortable fortune. She drove a four-horse freighting outfit up the pass by day, and by night made apple pie in dishes hammered out of old tin cans." (159)

Harriet Pullen was still there when we arrived in 1926 and continued to live in Skagway until her death in 1947. She owned and managed one of the town's two hotels, appropriately called The Pullen House—the largest hotel in Alaska when she established it in 1900.[5] In 1926 she was still a tall, handsome woman, in her mid-sixties, stylish, imposing in manner, a ready talker. On the rare occasions when we

---

[5] I am indebted to Carl Nord for this information, taken from the collection of brief biographies of Skagway folks that he kindly sent me.

Harriet Pullen

took our Sunday dinner at the Pullen House, she presided grandly over the dining room. During the summer, when tourists came to her hotel, she sometimes wore a "Days of '98" costume and fascinated her guests with tales of the Gold Rush days, some of which, I imagine, were actually true, including the saga of Soapy Smith. Some of her few surviving contemporaries, however, questioned the validity of her claim to have arrived as a widow and suggested that a husband had arrived with her and left some time after. One of her grandsons, Dan, stayed with her in Skagway for several years, for what reason I don't know. Dan and I became friends; but after he returned to his family in the States I never saw him again.

Women like Harriet Pullen were still too few to exercise their civilizing influence on the lawless town. Order, if any, was provided by one Jefferson Randolph Smith, a.k.a. Soapy Smith.

The legend of Soapy Smith and his nemesis Frank Reid was very much alive in 1926 (and thanks to its appeal to tourists it continues to the present day). The facts, briefly put, seem to be as follows.

Smith, who originally came from Georgia, cultivated the airs and appearance of a Southern gentleman, which served him well in his role as a con man. He probably acquired his name in Colorado, from his trick of fleecing the innocent by auctioning off bars of soap, many of which, he told his audience, contained a $100 bill. Indeed, after a few bars had been sold, a lucky buyer would triumphantly display the hundred-dollar bill he had just found beneath the wrapper of the soap. Naturally, many others would eagerly snap up the remaining bars as they were auctioned off. A few—enough to keep the scam going—might indeed contain the coveted bill. As you've already guessed, I'm sure, the lucky winners were his confederates.

Soapy employed innumerable scams and a great number of confederates, who in their search for victims roamed the town and sometimes even the White Pass. But woe to the victim who saw through the scam and tried to recover his money! Among their other duties, his confederates were also strict, swift, and brutal enforcers of Soapy's law. The law in Skagway, in short, was Soapy and his gang.[6]

Appropriately enough, Soapy's reign ended on July 4, 1898. He had cheated one time too often, and this time the victim insisted that he should get his money back. Perhaps by then the townspeople had had enough of Soapy and his ways.

A posse of vigilantes was formed. It was led by Frank Reid, the town surveyor, a one time schoolteacher and Indian fighter. In a scene that Hollywood could not have staged better, the posse gathered at the south end of town at the edge of the dock. Soapy, armed, headed toward them. They met. Although there are innumerable accounts of what happened, Berton's is wonderfully dramatic and probably the most accurate:

Soapy Smith in His Saloon

---

[6] It is interesting that the famous gold rush town of Dawson down the Yukon was in this respect completely different. The Mounties enforced law and order—even Sunday closings!—as new arrivals from Skagway who expected to find similar conditions in Dawson swiftly discovered.

"You can't go down there, Smith," Reid said.

Smith unslung the Winchester from his shoulder.

"Damn you, Reid," he said, "you're at the bottom of all my troubles. I should have got rid of you three months ago."

The two men were now almost nose-to-nose, and as Smith leveled the Winchester at Reid's head, Reid seized the muzzle with his left hand, pulling it downward, while he reached for the six-gun on his right.

"Don't shoot!" Smith cried, in sudden panic. "For God's sake, don't shoot!"

It was over in an instant.

Reid squeeze the trigger of his six-gun, but the hammer fell on a faulty cartridge, and an instant later a bullet from Smith's Winchester struck him in the groin, shattering his pelvic bone. Now both men fired again. Smith dropped to the dock, a bullet in his heart. Reid, wounded now in the leg, crumpled with him but fired again, striking the dying dictator in the left knee.[7]

Soapy died almost instantly. Reid lingered on for some days before he died.

Among the onlookers that day was Harriet Pullen. In later years she loved to entrance her audiences at the Pullen House with her eyewitness account of that fateful day. She was still doing so during our Skagway years.

But on that morning in January, 1926, when Mother, Lew, Roger, and I arrived in Skagway none of us, including Dad, knew the saga of Soapy Smith, or the town's turbulent early history.

Had we known, we all might have wondered whether it wasn't a horrible mistake to move from Inwood, Iowa, to this god-forsaken town in the mountainous wilds of Alaska.

---

[7] Berton, p. 359. Accounts differ somewhat. Carl Nord's biographies date Soapy Smith's death as July 8, Reid's as July 20.

3. Why We Moved to Skagway

After a month in the town, Dad must already have gained some confidence that the move from Inwood to Skagway would prove, with time, to have been a good idea. Still, as he stood on the wharf waving to us that January morning he may have been wondering whether Mother would ever forgive him for making her abandon the mid-West for the wilds of Alaska.

To understand her opposition to the move, I need to go back to their earlier life. She had been born in Canton, South Dakota, in 1889—the same year that two states, South Dakota and North Dakota, were carved out of Dakota Territory and admitted into the Union.

If earlier in her life Mother may have wanted to move away from the familiar area around Canton, these dreams had been extinguished, I think, by her two years living in Balf, a small town in Alberta, not far from Edmonton. That she was by no means lacking in a spirit of adventure is indicated by the fact that after two years at college in South Dakota she decided to take a job in a lawyer's office in Devil's Lake, North Dakota. She may even have entertained aspirations of becoming a lawyer. In her own way, she was, I think, something of a feminist. I don't think she ever doubted that women were as intelligent, resourceful, and competent as men. If she hadn't met and married Dad, it's possible she would have gone on to become a lawyer—though whether her life would have been more fulfilling than it turned out to be, I'm inclined (from my strongly biased perspective) to doubt.

It was while she was working in Devil's Lake that she met Dad.

Peter Ivarsen[8] Dahl was also a Midwesterner. His father Ivar Dahl (my grandfather) was the youngest of six sons born at the family farm

---

[8] Until he was an adult, Dad believed that his full name was simply Peter I., just the initial there in the middle, no more. On returning home one day in later years, possibly at his father's death in 1925, he discovered his full name in the family bible.

situated at the edge of a fjord some 100 kilometers northwest of Trondheim and called Dahl Vestre, or West Dahl, as it still is today. As the youngest, Ivar evidently saw no chance of acquiring a farm for himself and emigrated to America in 1865, first to Wisconsin for a brief period and then on to the Dakota Territory, a large tract of almost empty land (population 4837 in 1860).[9] Like the Norwegian immigrants to South Dakota in 1873 described by Otto Rölvaag in his novel *Giants in the Earth*, to make it through the harsh Dakota climate he built a sod hut, in which he lived at least for the first winter. Thanks to the recently enacted Homestead Act, he was able to acquire 160 acres of rich bottom land along the Red River, and later, as a result of a subsequent Act of Congress, he gained a further 160 acres (colloquially known as a "tree claim") by planting trees on the prairie land.

His oldest son, Peter, was born on the farm. Peter's first language, he said later, was Norwegian: he learned English at school. Lacking the least interest in becoming a farmer, he chose medicine instead. I find it interesting that, with one exception, all of Peter's siblings entered into the professions: one of his brothers became a lawyer, a second became a dentist, and of his three sisters one was a nurse and two were schoolteachers. Only Holbert, the youngest son, stayed on and ultimately ran the farm. Whether by cutting loose from the centuries' old ancestral tradition of farming Peter formed a role model for his brothers and sisters, or whether they were all encouraged by their father to leave farming for the professional world beyond, or, as I suspect, both, I do not know. I do know that Dad always spoke of his father in warm and affectionate terms, from which I have concluded that by rejecting farming, and perhaps by example encouraging the others to do so, he caused no breach with his father, and for all I know may have increased his admiration.

In any case, Peter attended the University of North Dakota and medical school at Northwestern University, interned in Chicago, and began his own medical practice in Devil's Lake. It was there that he met the legal secretary, Vera Lewis, there that he courted her, and there that he won her heart forever. On June 4, 1912, they were married in Canton. They returned to Devil's Lake.

The I stood for Ivarsen, the son of Ivar—which, given the Scandinavian naming system, seemed perfectly obvious once he saw it.

[9] In 1870, North Dakota, not yet a state, had a total population of 2,405. Along with South Dakota, Montana, and Washington, it became a state in 1889.

Vera continued working in the lawyer's office, despite some resistance from her new husband. Evidently the small town could scarcely provide enough patients for the new doctor in town. As Mother often told the story to us in later years, Dad protested one day that it was unseemly for the wife of a physician to be working.

"People will think," he said, "that I can't adequately support you on my income."

"Well," she replied, "you can't!"

When Peter learned that a hospital in the small town of Balf, near Edmonton in Alberta, needed a physician, he jumped at the chance. To Vera the move may have appealed to her youthful sense of adventure and promised an income sufficient to allow them to start a family.

Which they did. Their first son was born in Balf on December 11, 1914. For obvious reasons he was given the name Lewis. His second name is less self-evident. I'm pretty certain that Peter never gave a moment's thought to following Norwegian practice and calling him, say, Lewis Petersson Dahl. Instead, they chose the name of Kitchener, a choice that needs some explaining.

The First World War broke out in August, 1914, not long after they arrived in Balf. Had they foreseen it, they probably would not have moved. But here they now were, in a country at war. On the other side of the border, Americans were steadfastly neutral, as their president firmly announced to the world. Many Canadians found America's conduct despicable and, I imagine, sometimes said as much. I can recall Mother and Dad saying that, torn by their loyalty to their own country and their sympathies for the people among whom they now lived, they began to feel deeply uncomfortable. Meanwhile the British Secretary for War, Lord Kitchener, had become a popular hero in Britain and Canada because of his efforts to mobilize the Empire for the struggle. In a gesture of support, when Lew was born a few months after the outbreak of the Great War, Mother and Dad named their first-born son Lewis Kitchener. Although in later years the choice seemed an odd one, and Lew never much cared much for his middle name, he saw no reason to change it.[10]

---

[10] A confession. I had always believed that the choice of the name was stimulated by the surge of popular emotion in Britain and Canada after Kitchener drowned when the cruiser on which he was travelling was sunk by a German submarine in, as I thought, the first months of the War. Upon consulting two encyclopedias, I

It was after I was on the way, I believe, that they decided their other children should be born in the United States. By a stroke of luck, as it must have seemed at the time, one of Mother's uncles, Dave Lewis,[11] *was a physician practicing in Inwood, Iowa. I don't know what correspondence went on between Balf and Inwood, but the outcome was that Dad was invited to join him there. Exactly when they returned I do not know, but the records confirm that I was born in Inwood, Iowa, on December 17, 1915.*

I have always thought that despite the Canadian venture—or misadventure—Dad retained a bit of wanderlust, perhaps a throwback to his Viking ancestors. But once they were settled in Inwood, which was only eight miles from Canton, just across the state line, Mother was home. That was what she called it: home

Her parents still lived in the family house in Canton. Mother had no sisters and growing up with four brothers she had been much doted on. She felt great affection for them all, especially the youngest, Wilfred, the "baby" of her family during her girlhood. Wilfed lived in Canton, and another brother, Ray, lived with his family on a farm just outside the town. Art, a druggist like his father, was not far away in Sioux Falls, while Harry, a lawyer, twice married, and in family lore something of a cut-up, lived in the Black Hills.

Because Canton was so close we frequently visited her family, sometimes going by car, sometimes by the more exciting form of travel provided by a spur of the Milwaukee Railroad. Lew and I, and even the baby Roger, born in 1922, came to know the Lewis family, our grandparents, uncles, aunts, cousins and all. (Vera's father, James Lewis, died a year before we left Inwood.)

Inwood and Canton: here was the small, familiar part of the world to which she had returned and where she knew she really belonged.

After Balf, Mother was finished with moving. Or at least so she thought.

But there was a fly in the ointment, a big one. The War created a huge demand for food, and an agricultural bubble. Prices shot up. Iowa

---

now find to my astonishment that his death from drowning *occurred in June 1916* after the cruiser hit a German mine off the Orkney's. So much for family legends and oral history.

[11] I had remembered his name as Will, but according to a family tree supplied by a Lewis cousin, Will was a lawyer in Iowa, John was an M.D. in Canton, and Dave was the M.D. in Inwood.

farmers became exceptionally prosperous. Dad invested in land, naturally. Then as bubbles do sooner or later, this one collapsed.

In 1915, the year I was born, wheat was $1.29 a bushel. By 1920 it reached an astronomical $2.45. The next year—the year before Roger was born—the price fell to almost half: $1.32. In 1915, one head of hog fetched, on average, $9.95; by1919, hog prices had more than doubled, to $22.18; in 1921 they crashed to $13.63 and three years later they were at $10.30. In 1915, a hundred pounds of pork sold at wholesale for $6.47; by 1920, their price had doubled to $13.91. One year later, the pork market collapsed all the way down to $8.51 a hundred weight.

In short, we moved to Inwood at the start of an agricultural boom caused by the food demands of World War I. The boom peaked in 1920, and crashed the next year. The agricultural depression in and around Iowa was still very much with us in 1925.

Of course, people were just as likely as ever to get sick, they still called on the doctor for help, and Dad, always a conscientious physician, went. As best I can tell, he and his partner Dave Lewis pretty much split the practice: Dave kept the town, Dad had the farmers in the countryside.

I've never known whether Dave felt put upon by accepting Dad into his practice. Did he invite Dad into partnership in response to Mother's importuning letters asking him to help them leave Balf? Did he share some of the prevailing prejudice that folks of English and Scottish ancestry felt toward the Scandinavians—the "dumb Swedes" of so many jokes? I don't know. I do have faint and uncertain memories of later accounts by Mother and Dad of a bad relationship, of suspicions that Dave had falsified the accounts to take more money from the partnership than was his due, even a lawsuit.

What is certain is that Dad had a large practice in the countryside. He was not only conscientious, as I've said. He spoke Norwegian fluently, and that would have been a plus for many of the Scandinavian farmers. He could talk with them in their own language, or in the case of Swedes and Danes one close enough for mutual understanding. When he was needed, he went, in all hours and in all weather, including the sometimes harsh winter days and nights. In his more prosperous period before the agricultural bubble collapsed he had bought a touring car, a Dodge, I think. Why he chose a touring car, I don't know, but in good weather it seemed quite spiffy. It had, as I remember, a top and sides of canvas, with Isinglass windows. (Today, who's ever heard of Isinglass?)

The Dodge provided him with the means to make his calls to the farmers out in the country. His practice was, I think, quite large, and during the bubble period of prosperity it must have provided a fair income. But when the bubble broke the farmers had scarcely enough income to pay their most urgent bills, not least their mortgages. Traditionally, doctors' bills came last, and my father was never one to put his fee before his service. He was, in fact, a poor businessman who so hated sending out bills that in Skagway, for patients who weren't employees of the railroad, Mother finally took over the task of bill collecting—to the relief, I'm sure, of both Mother and Dad.

The house in which I was born, one of the finest in Inwood, could no longer be afforded. So we moved to the house that I still remember well. By any standards, and certainly by the standards Mother had assumed growing up in their comfortable house in Canton, it was a dismal structure. It was located on the northwestern edge of town, facing a pasture to the north and an alfalfa field just two or three houses beyond us on the east. Our only source of water in the house was a pump in the kitchen that drew from a well below. The water was unsafe to drink, and it became a daily chore assigned to Lew and me to go to the outdoor pump of our friendly next-door neighbor, bucket in hand, to draw our drinking water. Our only toilet facility was a wooden outhouse fifty feet from our back door, a standard two-holer. The kitchen range on which Mother did the cooking and baking and heated the water for washing clothes and bathing was fueled by corncobs. Since a corncob is about as poor a steady fuel as a rolled up newspaper, the stove required a huge supply. The corncobs, which were supplied by some farmer in lieu of cash with which to pay his medical bill, were piled in a corner of the barn where Dad kept the Dodge. One of the daily chores assigned to Lew and me was to keep the large washtub next to the kitchen stove full of corncobs.

Failing to perform that necessary chore resulted in the only spanking by my father that I can now remember. When Lew and I arrived home from school one afternoon Mother was cooking bread, as she did several times a week to keep us adequately supplied. The washtub was empty, and she asked us to fill it immediately, before the fire went out and the bread was ruined. We began to argue: Whose turn was it, Lew's or mine? Mother pleaded, the fire burned low, we continued to argue, Mother pleaded further. The fire went out. The bread was ruined. Mother was furious. She cried. We had already grown too big for her to spank, something she had almost never done anyway. So when Dad came home, she told him what had happened. For our egregious failure he gave us each a licking, which he hated to do. It didn't amount to much. But we never again failed in our duty to keep the washtub full. (And I sometimes think it helped us both to build a sense of responsibility.)

Despite Dad's large practice, he had little cash income. The farmers were too poor to pay the doctor in cash. Yet we never went hungry, for they paid their doctor's bills in kind: a year's supply of fresh eggs, say, and milk, cream, butter, a joint of beef, a hog butchered and dressed, chickens, maybe a duck, an occasional goose, fresh vegetables, potatoes, corn, apples, peaches, pears . . .

But buying a new pair of shoes or pants was something else. Every purchase that required cash became a major challenge for the household budget.

Whether it was because of the year's difference in our ages, or because Lew was the first and eldest, or because he was more sensitive in some ways than I, or all of these, I don't know, but in later years when we compared our memories of this bleak period I seem to have passed through it without much awareness of our desperate poverty while Lew was very conscious of it.

For poverty it was. And surely it was not what either Dad or Mother had ever expected—Dad who had escaped the hard life of a farmer for a career in an esteemed and well-rewarded profession, Mother who had grown up in pleasant circumstances in Canton, where her family always had a maid or two and lived, by the small town standards of the time, in relative ease and affluence. In marrying Dad she could never have anticipated that she might one day live in this degree of poverty, drudgery, and hardship.

Yet when the opportunity came to leave that all behind, she was the one who balked.

As she would relate the story in later years, in the fall of 1925 Dad revealed that a railway in Alaska was advertising for a physician who would care for the railroad employees and be paid a regular salary. He wanted to apply for the post. To get away from all this hard work for both of them, and no money.

Mother was aghast. She said something along these lines:

"After our experience in Balf, you still have the nerve to ask me to move to another god-forsaken part of the world? Alaska? I just won't hear of it, and I don't want you to talk to me about such foolishness ever again!"

In mid-November or thereabouts Dad came home one day and announced that he had decided to accept the position and they had already sent the tickets.

"What?" Mother said. "What position?"

"The one I told you about, the one in Alaska, a town called Skagway. I'll be the physician for the railroad there. I'll have a salary, a regular income."

"But I told you never to talk to me about that job again!"

"Well," Dad said, "I didn't."

Mother vowed she wouldn't go. But I think Dad knew her well enough to know she could be persuaded. He said he would go on ahead, look the town over, find a house, and then if all seemed fine send the tickets for the rest of us.

His report must have been enough to persuade Mother. When the tickets came in mid-December, we made one last visit to Canton and got on the train for Seattle.

And here we were.

4. Pansies in Winter

Almost as soon as the gangplank was laid down, Dad came aboard. Our long month of separation ended with hugs. Though my memory of the event has dimmed with time, I imagine that despite Dad's acute embarrassment about demonstrating his affections in public, Mother managed to extract not only a hug but a kiss as well.

I know that we were all impatient to see what Skagway was like. Our luggage had been ready to go for an hour or more. We and it were soon stowed in the car—which served as the town's one and only taxi—that Dad had arranged to carry us from the boat up the long dock and then to the Golden North Hotel.

I have often wondered what thoughts may have been whirling through his mind as we drove to the hotel. I'm sure he saw Skagway as our big chance to escape the poverty in which we had existed in Inwood. Yet because he was deeply devoted to his family, and our happiness meant everything to him—more, probably, even than his beloved profession—he must have been greatly concerned about what we would think of Skagway, and, who knows? maybe what Skagway would think of us.

Though Mother was not excessively demanding, I'm dead certain she had hopes for a more satisfactory life than their struggles in Iowa had provided. To be sure, their marriage was strong; in fact, the two rarely quarreled and I believe their love was secure. In fact, when we taped an interview with her on her ninetieth birthday she claimed that after a spat early in their marriage they had never quarreled again. This, I know, was untrue; her memory, which up until a few years earlier had been extraordinarily sharp, was no longer fully reliable. Yet I think her recollection revealed an essential truth about their marriage. Basically, even in the midst of poverty they were deeply and forever in love with one another.

But because Dad was greatly concerned with her happiness, and his children's, he might well have wondered: What would she think about moving to Skagway? What would his boys think of the town?

The answers were far from clear. If Skagway was now in a contest with Inwood for our favorable opinions, maybe in Mother's view Inwood, despite its defects, began a good number of points ahead. Inwood, after all, was close to family and friends. And at least it was a part of the known world, the civilized world. Was Skagway?

One aspect of our arrival was not altogether auspicious. On the way north through the fjords of the Inside Passage we had noticed that, contrary to what you might expect in January, the sun seemed to rise somewhat later each day. Between the increasing latitude and the mountainous barriers to the sun's rays, the sun arrived later than we were accustomed to in Iowa, even in December. By the time we reached the Golden North that morning, the sun had not yet risen above the crest of the mountain ridge to the East.

Luckily, any negative impressions produced by our first encounter with longer winter nights than we were accustomed to were soon offset. When the sun finally came up over the mountain in midmorning it highlighted a sky that was blue from crest to crest on every side. What is more, the weather was mild, well above freezing, maybe in the fifties. I don't know quite what kind of climate we'd expected, but I imagine we had pictured it as somewhere between a frigid Iowa winter and a long Arctic night when frequent blizzards blew relentlessly across an endless expanse of ice and snow. And here it was practically spring! Mercifully, at that time none of us, including Dad, knew that the winter of '26 was one of the warmest on record, in Skagway at least. We were never to see its like again.

But because we didn't know that, in the competition between Skagway and Inwood, Skagway had just scored some points.

But would Skagway prove to be a social barrens? In fact, we hadn't yet learned that Skagway couldn't even qualify as a one-horse town—the closest horse was the one in Dyea. And when you got right down to it, Skagway was definitely just a one-*car* town. Ignoring one or two bashed up trucks, the taxi that carried us to the Golden North was the town's one and only automobile. As I remember, it was used mainly for deliveries from the main grocery store, Ask's, though it did extra duty as an occasional taxi and, on the rare occasions when it was needed, as a hearse.

The Golden North was the largest building in town, a two-story structure made of wood built a quarter century earlier during the expansive Gold Rush period. By 1926 it was a bit scruffy, though certainly tolerable. Anyway, we didn't much care, because we would stay at the hotel only a day or so, until we had moved into the house that Dad had rented. On hotels, probably no points were scored on either side.

The Tropea House

After lunch at the Golden North we walked the ten blocks to the Tropea House, as we always called it. It was owned by the Tropeas, who with their two daughters lived over their bakery on Broadway.

Painted white, like most of the other houses in Skagway it was constructed of wood and was probably built before 1910. It was surrounded on three sides by an attractive white picket fence with a gate swinging in from the wooden sidewalk.

As we opened the gate we were greeted with an unbelievable sight. Along each side of the walkway to the house, pansies were in bloom! Those pansies racked up a good many points for Skagway. As Mother confessed in later years, it was at this moment that she began to think that the move to Skagway might not be quite as bad as she had feared.

Then came what could well prove to be the most crucial factor, the house itself. The small open porch led to a vestibule that opened into a room running the depth of the house that would serve adequately as a living room and dining area. On one side, a door opened to a full-length bedroom that Mother and Dad would occupy; the other, to a kitchen. Wonder of wonders! The kitchen stove was fueled by coal. No more corn cobs. Even better, the coal was supplied by the railroad and was dirt cheap.

At one corner of the kitchen a door led into the only bathroom. And lo! The bathroom had a hot water tank that was fueled by electricity—which, as it turned out, was also dirt cheap. Our next door neighbors, Mr. and Mrs. Nye, owned and operated the power company where turbines were driven by an endless source of water plunging down the steep mountain side. An electric hot water heater! Yet another plus for Skagway: with the turn of a tap we could drink pure water drawn from the Reservoir six hundred feet up the mountain. No more foul water from the kitchen pump, no more filling a pail from the neighbor's well, no more having to heat water on the kitchen range for bathing and for washing clothes.

At the other corner of the kitchen, a door led to a small pantry that contained a washing machine and some shelves. (In later years, Mother would try in vain to hide in that pantry some of the fresh doughnuts she had just cooked, to prevent the rest of us from eating every last one that very day. Mind you, we all rather liked doughnuts that were a day or two old. But we rarely exercised enough self-restraint to have any.)

The points for Skagway were piling up.

At the end of the dining room, stairs led up to a second floor with a small room for Roger and beyond it another that was just big enough for a double bed in which Lew and I would sleep.

So far so good. But a black monstrous object shaped like an unusually large barrel stood between the living room and dining area. Its function was revealed by a black pipe coming out the top. It was a stove—not your standard heater with fancy stainless steel hardware, but a plain unadorned tin-roofing sort of affair with no hardware at all. As we were to learn, it had been made by a machinist at the railroad shops from a piece of sheet-metal around an eighth of an inch thick. In the ceiling above the stove we could see a transom to what would be Roger's bedroom: that transom was how the upstairs would be heated by the stove below. Aside from the kitchen range and the electric water heater, this barrel-like stove would be the only source of heat in the house.

Unlike the kitchen range, this stove burned wood—ten to twelve cords of it a year, we were to discover. Spruce, pine, and hemlock trees that grew abundantly along the railroad trucks were cut into eighteen inch lengths, hauled down in a boxcar, and dumped in the alley next to our house. Opening into the alley, beyond the pantry of the Tropea house, was a shed. Its main function was to store the firewood. One of the annual chores that Lew and I would share, though happily we weren't aware of it at the time of our arrival, was to carry those ten or so cords of wood from the alley into the shed. Not only that. The daily chores rotating between Lew and me would also include splitting the chunks for kindling, arising first each winter morning to start the fire in that stove, and insuring a steady supply of wood stowed at a safe distance behind the stove.

Despite the unattractive living room stove, and modest as the house was, in comparison with that dismal place back in Inwood it was a notable improvement. The Tropea house, I'd guess, scored a lot of points right off for Skagway.

Skagway had still one more advantage, one that Inwood couldn't meet: Dad's salary. He would be employed by the Railroad at a steady salary of $250 a month, year around. Nowadays three thousand a year sounds like a trifle, but in 1926 it would provide a comfortable living for a family of five. Here's one way to think about it. In 1939, the recently created Consumer Price Index was measured at 13.9; in 1997 it was 160.5. To put the comparison over-simply, in 1997 it would take you $160 in 1997 dollars to buy the rough equivalent of what, in 1939, you could buy for fourteen bucks! Using these equivalents, if Dad's annual salary in 1926 were converted to its 1997 equivalent it would come to about $35,000. Not only that: although Dad couldn't charge Railroad employees for his services, because they were entitled to free medical care (shades of socialized medicine!), he could charge patients who didn't work for the railroad, who would mainly consist of the other residents in the town plus the occasional tourist stricken with an illness or, even more rarely, someone from the nearest towns, Haines and Whitehorse. How much these private patients added to his income I don't know for sure, but I would guess another third.

Consider also that in those days our *expectations* were far lower than those of an American middle class or professional family today. Our basic wants, you might say, were far closer to our basic needs. According to our own standards and those of the people around us, we could live quite well on what Dad made. A social psychologist might say today that we enjoyed "*relative* affluence."

Now add in one more crucial element: his income was regular and certain. No more not knowing where the next dollar was coming from, when indeed it came at all. No more depending on patients who had to pay their medical bills with meat and butter and chickens and eggs.

Dad's income, the house, the lucky draw on the weather, all might have been enough to tip the balance strongly in Skagway's favor except for several unknown factors that might yet tip the balance toward Inwood. For one, what could we expect in the way of friends for Mother, Dad, Lew, Roger, and me? For another, would the school be adequate? What would our lives really be like?

In short, just what kind of town *was* Skagway?

5. The Town

In 1930, the total population Skagway was 492, according to the U.S. Census. Give or take a few changes as a result of births and deaths, that was about what it was in 1926.

In 1930 the population of the entire Territory of Alaska was 59,000, only a few thousand more than it had been in 1920. The Territory was spread over 586,000 square miles—nearly one-fifth the size of the rest of the U.S., as Alaskans like to point out—which works out to just about ten square miles per person. But probably around 99% of those ten square miles per person were uninhabited by human beings. They were composed of mountains, forests, glaciers, rivers, lakes, seas, and tundra, and inhabited by coyotes, wolves, wolverines, grizzlies, brown, black and polar bears, moose, caribou, deer, mountain goats, Bighorn sheep, porcupines, marmots, and endless numbers of grey squirrels and jackrabbits, not to mention mosquitoes and no-see-ums that in legendary millions launched their vicious attacks on the unwary human intruder.

Of the 59 thousand or so human souls uncovered by Census takers, most lived in small towns or even tinier villages. Like other Alaskans, we called Skagway a town; most Americans, I presume, would have called it a village. Even the largest town, Juneau, which was the capital then as it is today, was actually little more than a village: it had about five thousand residents.

Alaskans were almost evenly divided between Whites and Native Americans, who were predominantly Inuit, then universally called Eskimo by others, living above the Arctic Circle, and Athabaskan or Tlingit Indians. (Unable to pronounce the plosive beginning, whites called them Klinkits.) Reflecting Alaska's recent frontier origins, males outnumbered females 3-2. For an unmarried woman looking for a spouse, Alaska was a promising place, as women teachers and nurses quickly discovered if they hadn't known it all along.

The District of which Skagway was an official part, if only for Census purposes, also included Haines (pop. 344), Chilkoot Barracks (U. S. Army, pop. 234), and the native village of Klukwan (pop. 97). In our day, Skagway folk looked down on Haines as a rundown backwater.

The roles were briefly reversed when the Alaska Highway was built during World War II. Haines became a major entry point, while postwar Skagway went into a drastic slump.

In the District of Skagway, Whites numbered 853, Tlingit Indians 390, some of whom spoke little or no English. I'd guess that in Skagway itself the Tlingits numbered less than a hundred, let's say about one out of five.

The Town of Skagway

There was a perfectly good reason why Skagway was a no-horse, one-car town in 1926. Completely hemmed in by the sea and the mountains, the only roads it needed were its own streets. These were laid out in the standard grid pattern common in the West and Midwest, which divided the town into rectangular blocks around a hundred by a hundred and fifty yards square. The four longest streets ran straight north-south, were less than a mile long, and bore names of striking unoriginality. The one named

Broadway we usually called "Downtown" because it was where the shops and stores were located. The two mainly residential streets were named State and Main. Although a fourth street, which during an unusual burst of creativity had been named "Alaska," ran, in theory, next to the edge of the wide and rocky riverbed of the Skagway River, in fact Alaska Street existed mostly on town maps.

Much of the time, if you stood on the tidal flats and faced north siting a rifle along State or Main, you could have fired a shot all the way to the other end without hurting a soul. As far as I know, however, no one ever tried.

Cutting athwart these North-South streets, running from the riverbank on the West almost to the base of the mountains on the East, were a dozen or so numbered streets, which with no little exaggeration were called avenues. These began at First Avenue on the south edge of the town, not far from the tidal flats that swept down to the Bay, and continued at regular intervals up to Twelfth or thereabouts at the North end of town.

So if you drove a car up and down each of the streets you would cover altogether about three miles. If you were crazy enough to continue and traverse all the avenues as well, you might pile up a grand total of approximately six miles, hardly a fine Sunday drive with the wife and kids. To my knowledge, no one in Skagway was ever *quite* that crazy—or at least not crazy enough in exactly *that* way. Consequently, no one saw much need for a car.

It wasn't until after I'd left home for college that a road was built to Dyea and another was blasted out for a few miles along the base of AB Mountain. Thanks to these new roads, short as they were, people began to conclude that a family car might be nice to have after all.

For most people, walking would do. Summer and winter, the wooden sidewalks served us well enough. If you were careful about the very few loose or broken planks, the sidewalks were even satisfactory for biking. Taken all in all, then, streets and sidewalks were all that Skagway really needed.

❦

Still, if you were coming fresh from Iowa, you might feel isolated at times, maybe even rather hemmed in by those formidable mountains.

The nearest town, Haines, and its next door neighbor Chilkoot Barracks, where a battalion of soldiers was stationed, were about 15 miles away and could be reached only by boat. For some years an old converted minesweeper called the Fornance made the roundtrip between Haines and Skagway once a month or so, but few Skagway people had any reason to make the trip. The next nearest town, Whitehorse in Yukon Territory, was 110 miles to the North, at the northern terminus of the White Pass and Yukon Route Railway. The locomotive engineers, firemen, and trainmen, who all lived in Skagway, would make the trip to Whitehorse several times a week, summer and winter, usually staying overnight in a cabin they'd acquired just for that purpose. The rest of us, however, rarely went to Whitehorse. One exception was during the Christmas holidays, when two hockey teams, men's and boys', might take the train to Whitehorse to contest the ice with their teams, which, more often than not, beat ours. After all, they were not only Canadians, who as everyone knew were *born* with ice skates on their feet, but in Whitehorse *they* had ice from October until April whereas in Skagway our outdoor rink didn't usually freeze until December and then melted in March.

Skagway's connections to Vancouver and Seattle and from there to the rest of the world—we called it "the Outside"—were minimal. Neither telephone nor radio linked Skagway to the Outside world.

In the late 'twenties a few people acquired radios that were enormous in size—I seem to remember the name Super Heterodyne—and pitifully weak in their capacity to receive radio signals. Because Seattle stations were a thousand miles away and radio signals were blocked by the mountains around us, a Super Heterodyne's proud owner had to turn up the volume to ear-splitting levels. Even then heavy static blotted out the announcer's words, especially during the winter months when Northern lights created their own noisy and decidedly unmusical interference *("Music of the Spheres," bah, humbug.)* We soon learned not to put much trust in the garbled reports passed on us by the owner of a radio.

If you really had to, you could send a cable. Some time around the First World War, the Army had laid a cable to Seattle, to connect Chilkoot Barracks, I suppose, just in case the Army's assistance was needed. (It never was, so far as I know.) The cable had been extended to Skagway. So it was possible to send or receive a cable, if the need arose.

Telephone service was strictly local. You cranked a wall phone to reach "Central," who was usually spoken to by her name:

"Oh, Dorothy, it's you. And how is little Georgie today? Better? Would you please ring Tropea's store? I want to see if they have any fresh bread today."

Among other things, Central could help to track down Dad if he were neither at home nor the Hospital.

"Oh, Mabel, they need Doctor at the Hospital. They say he left there about ten minutes ago. Would you try the barbershop?

(Two minutes later.) "Oh, he left there five minutes ago? Try Keller's drug store, would you please?"

Skagway was visibly connected to the Outside, however, during the summer. From about mid-June to the end of August, tourists boats from Vancouver (Canadian Pacific or Canadian National) and Seattle (the Alaska Line) flooded the town with tourists. After the tourist boats stopped at summer's end we regained our town and lost immediate touch with the rest of the world. From late August until early June our connection with the Outside was a boat every two weeks or so that brought mail, newspapers, magazines, food, and other supplies.

※

In its heyday Skagway had had its own newspaper, but long before we arrived it had disappeared. After all, how could a town of five hundred support its own newspaper?

The best we could do was to subscribe to one of the two Seattle papers, the *Post-Intelligencer* or the *Times*. The *Post-Intelligencer*, or P. I., as it was usually called, was a Hearst paper. Early in his life, Dad had come to detest William Randolph Hearst and all that he and his newspapers stood for. Later, following FDR's election in 1932, when the reactionary Hearst papers steadily attacked Dad's hero, what had been mere detestation moved to a higher stage of loathing and fury. But even in the days of Coolidge and Hoover, Dad wouldn't let the P. I. into our house. The Seattle *Times*, though editorially on the conservative side, was a sober and well-edited newspaper, then as later. So we subscribed to the *Times*.

During the nine month period when the boats arrived at two week intervals, we would receive our fourteen days of the *Times* in one big batch. I can imagine Dad picking up his two weeks supply at the Post Office, glancing at a headline, and making an observation to Martin Conway, the Postmaster. Mr. Conway, who had been born in Ireland, arrived in Skagway from Seattle in 1898 and was appointed postmaster by Woodrow Wilson, from which I'd guess he was, like Dad, a Democrat.[12] So they might have had a brief and amicable discussion about politics. Dad was not one, however, to hide his political beliefs, and I can imagine moments when his comments may have produced a lively discussion among people picking up their newly arrived two weeks of mail.

However that may be, he would arrive home with fourteen days of the Seattle *Times*. Having deposited his precious two week of newspapers on a table, Dad would read one each day. By the time the next batch arrived two weeks later, he was, so to speak, perfectly up-to-date. You might think that the news was already stale. But given our lack of communication with the Outside, each days news in the *Times* was perfectly fresh. Strange as it may seem to people who are accustomed, as we all are nowadays, to getting their "news as it happens," we didn't mind. That it was to weeks old mattered not at all. For us, after all, it was news.

❦

Did we feel isolated? Bored? Obviously I can't speak for everyone, but my guess is that most of us weren't bored. Except for some of the merchants whose business was mainly with tourists—Kirmse's and Richter's—most of us, I think, were glad to have our town back in September. I'm pretty sure that was true of my parents and certain it was true for Lew, Roger, and me.

As I'll describe later, for most of us, younger and older, the seasons of fall, winter, and spring were a busy, active, social time.

❦

Are these just the tender, romantic, somewhat falsified memories of old age? A little, no doubt. But at base they are, I believe, essentially true.

Still, I must admit that when I came to know Skagway well, and, much later, had time to reflect on what I knew and didn't know or didn't want to think about, I discovered a community more complex than the town I've described so far. Partly obscured my warm and bright memories, I realized, the town also had a darker side.

---

[12] Here, as in later chapters, I have drawn freely on the biographical sketches in Carl Nord's collection of family histories.

6. Who Were They?

They flooded in from America and Europe. As I imagine them now, they would have been pressed forward by an assortment of reasons and motives: the prospect of sudden riches, greed, a wish to escape the narrow limits of their lives, fear, hope, threat, adventure, challenge, opportunities for sex and marriage, and, like lemmings drawn irresistibly along with the moving mass of their fellow creatures, the contagious spread of a herd mentality.

❁

Even the earliest gold seekers were newcomers, as the Russians and other explorers had been before them. Alaska and the Yukon were home to people whose ancestors had been around for several thousand years and more. In Southeast Alaska, these were the Tlingit Indians. For the moment, though, I'm going to put the Indians to one side. Considerably before we arrived in town, they had already been shoved aside by the white invaders of their ancient lands, who then shoved them further, down to the very bottom of the heap. I'll have more to say about the Tlingits, what I knew about them then, and what I didn't know or understand or want to know until many years later.

❁

Most of those who came North were carried back on the receding tide, their hopes dashed, their spirit of adventure overwhelmed by harsh reality. Yet a tiny number stayed on in the towns and villages of Alaska and the Yukon. For some of these, Skagway was the northern terminus of their journey. Others drifted south from Dawson, the Klondike, and Whitehorse, or abandoned the ghost town Dyea, and finally stopped moving when they reached Skagway.

WHO WERE THEY?

By the time we arrived in January, 1926, the heroes and scoundrels of the Gold Rush like Captain Moore, Soapy Smith, Frank Reid were long gone, though their legends lived on, bigger than life. Yet like Harriet Pullen, twenty or more residents who had arrived during the peak Gold Rush years from 1896 to 1899 were still around. They ranged in age from Mrs. Pullen and George Rapuzzi, Sr., both 62, down to George Rapuzzi, Jr., who had been born in Skagway in 1899. George Dedman, Sr., an 1898 arrival, had died a few years before we came to Skagway, but his widow, Clara, was a vigorous and active 61. Their son, born in 1899, they named Henry Alaska thereby honoring both his father and the Territory of Alaska, their new home. He was, they noted later, the second white child born in Skagway.

About half the surviving settlers from 1897-99 were over 50. Viewed from my youthful perspective, they were real old-timers. Another three dozen or so had arrived during the boom years from 1900 to 1910. By the time we arrived in 1926, then, probably around one out of six white people in Skagway had been there since 1910 or earlier.[13]

We were newcomers.

❈

Like those who had come and left, the ones who stayed had started life in many different places. George Rapuzzi, who reached Skagway in 1897 from Seattle, had been born in Genoa around 1860. (We never knew him: he had died in 1922). Like George, his wife Theresa had also been born in Genoa in 1860, and when we arrived "Ma" Rapuzzi was still a vigorous woman of 63 who continued to manage her fruit and vegetable store and keep tabs on her large and industrious family. Charlie Peterson, a 1904 arrival, and Hans Soldin, who came a year before we did, were both from Sweden. The seniors of the large Selmer family, Oscar and Paula, came from Oslo; Chris Larsen from Norway; George Brown from Ireland; Ken Hannan from Jamaica; his wife Muriel, or "Dusty," who would become one of Mother's dearest friends, from London. Ysoult Farwell[14] had been born in Essex, England. Fred and Anna Story had come from Gloucester,

---

[13] I have made these estimates from the biographies in the valuable collection assembled by Carl Nord.

[14] I had never known her exotic first name until I discovered it in the Nord Collection. Her son Bill once claimed that she had worked in the Royal Household. Soon

Massachusetts. Father Gallant, who was to play an important role in my education, hailed originally from Prince Edward Island. Other Skagwayites had come from West Virginia, Minnesota, Washington, California, wherever....

❊

The natives to one side, ethnic diversity was not very significant. The preponderant bulk of the people were North American or North European. Ma Rapuzzi retained her strong Italian accent, as did the other couple of Italian origin, the Tropeas.[15] I don't doubt that people were sometimes amused by the heavily accented American-English of Ma Rapuzzi and the elder Tropeas, or the Scandinavian lilt in the speech of Charlie Petersen, Hans Soldin, and Oscar Selmer, Sr. For all I know Martin Itjen may have put on his German accent a bit more thickly for the benefit of the tourists he drove in his "Street Car" up to Soapy Smith's grave at the far North end of town. My mother was sometimes charmed by her friend Dusty Hannan's English accent and word usage.

But the second generation Rapuzzis and Tropeas, were, in typical American fashion, thoroughly assimilated. To my knowledge none spoke Italian. So too with others, no matter where their parents or grandparents were born. As a result, I can't remember giving much thought to the ethnic origins of any of my schoolmates. Indeed, it was only some years after I had left Skagway and lived among people where ethnic diversities were more distinctive that I began to find ethnic differences interesting and sometimes worth noting. (Certainly I hadn't the faintest idea that some day I would learn to speak passable Italian and come to love its melodious sound in the mouth of a native Italian speaker.)

❊

Religious differences were somewhat more salient, though so far as I know they were not a major influence on friendships and social interactions. Skagway had two churches, one Presbyterian, one Catholic, though many

---

after we arrived, she started The Tea Room, which drew its clientele from women like my mother and her friends, and during summer from tourists.

[15] I haven't found any information about their birthplace or date of their arrival.

people attended neither. More people were, I think, nominally Protestant than Catholic, but I doubt whether church attendance differed by much.

When we arrived the Protestant minister was a man named Peterson—I've forgotten his first name. Lew and I immediately started attending Sunday School, as did most of our friends. Because Sunday School followed (or did it precede?) the regular church service, which we usually didn't attend, Reverend Peterson was able to take advantage of the opportunity to mold our youthful minds to his views. Whatever his hopes may have been for winning us around, Lew and I soon began to conclude that he was a man who combined ignorance with bigotry in about equal measures. It was impossible, we soon saw, to engage him in any serious discussion of matters that endangered his narrow beliefs. I don't doubt that we had grown altogether too accustomed to the wide-ranging discussions around the dinner table—as we said many years later, we discussed anything and everything, except money—and we may have foolishly assumed that Sunday School would allow us equal freedom. But after attending pretty faithfully for several years, and even acquiring the small medals that attested to our unbroken attendance records, we both began to chafe under his imperious dogmatism.

One Sunday, not perhaps altogether innocently, we undiplomatically brought up the question of evolution. Lew, who was more outspoken than I in taking on the minister, bore the burden of the defense. Peterson was, of course, apoplectic, which I suppose was a part of our secret agenda. By the time we arrived home after Sunday School that day, we'd decided that we would never go back. We so informed our parents, who readily accepted our decision—Dad, I think, with particular satisfaction not only because he heartily disliked Peterson but because our emerging views fitted with his own skepticism, or to put it more positively, his a-theistic humanism. Although Mother retained a tad more of her Protestantism than Dad, she supported our decision, as, in fact, she generally did.

Through an unrecorded miracle a few years later, Peterson was replaced by a new minister. His name was Warren Griffiths and he was as different from Peterson in every way as two people could be. Although he hailed from Ohio, he had been trained at that bastion of theological and political liberalism, the Union Theological Seminary in New York City. He was young, fresh out of Union Theological, small in stature, slender, good-looking, intelligent, well spoken. And liberal, politically and theologically. Because of his attractiveness, I can imagine that every youngish woman in town developed a bit of a crush on him; but it wasn't only the young women who were his admirers: the whole town became so. He entered into town activities with enthusiasm. A good sport and a good athlete, he played basketball in the winter, and, in the spring and summer, baseball (on an occasional Sunday afternoon, if I recall correctly). He tried to learn to play ice hockey, though he was, as I recall, pretty awkward on the ice. He joined the rest of us in hiking, fishing, town picnics, whatever. He even joined the young males who competed in contests for money prizes on the Fourth of July, when he ran and sometimes won the hundred-yard dash.

We all, young and old alike, called him Griff.

Griff soon became a close friend of our entire family. Mother, who had been turned off by Peterson, became somewhat more active again in Presbyterian Church affairs. Dad liked and admired Griff, but attending church was more than he was up for—which Griff, I think, fully understood.

Nor did Lew and I return to church. We were too old for Sunday School and not even Griffs' sermons, in which he gently urged his listeners to find a greater place in their lives for love, brotherhood, tolerance, and decency, could draw us back.

❈

After ten years or so, Griff left Skagway for a parish in Ohio. He married and had two children. One day when the whole family were driving in their car, an accident occurred in which his wife and two children were all killed. He left the ministry, gained a Ph. D. in political science, and joined the faculty of Wooster College in Oxford, Ohio. By chance, I ran into him once at an American Political Science Association meeting in New York. I happened to be president of the association. Over his hesitations I insisted that he join me for a lunch with assorted dignitaries in the profession. Griff was, I think, somewhat ill at ease. To my regret I never followed up the encounter, and I never ran into him again.

❈

Father Gallant, the Catholic priest, had come to Skagway in 1921, only a few years before our own arrival in Skagway. Born on Prince Edward

Island, as I mentioned earlier, he reached Skagway after a brief stint in Juneau. Now in 1926 he was thirty-two, tall (six feet two or three, I'd guess), handsome, articulate, impressive in manner and bearing, and highly sociable. Unlike Griff he didn't participate in the town's athletic activities, much less the winter dances at Elk's Hall. Yet he fitted easily into the town's informality. For example, he regularly played bridge with Mother and Dad—and, for that matter, joined them frequently in an evening of penny-ante poker, along with Hal Johnston, Sr., who was as outspoken in his anti-Catholicism as anyone in town, including my father. (I think Hal Senior actually called him Edgar, which, to my knowledge, no one else ever did.) After Prohibition was repealed in 1933 and a bar or two opened up on Broadway, Father G. would occasionally stroll in to one of them for a drink; though he was in no way a heavy drinker he was sociable and enjoyed company. Whether any of his parishioners thought the less of him for his ecumenical and socially liberal ways, I don't know, but I'm inclined to think they admired him as much as we did.

The second summer following our arrival, when I was 12 and Lew 13, Father Gallant led us on one of the most memorable adventures of our entire lives. A young Episcopalian minister, who was staying in Skagway for some time—just why, I don't recall—was eager to hike over the Trail of '97, the famous Chilkoot Pass. Three decades after the Chilkoot Pass was abandoned for White Pass Trail of '98, the old trail had become wholly unused even for adventure. It was overgrown in many places with thick stands of willow and alder and wiped out by rockslides and shifts in the course of the Dyea River. Though the Chilkoot Pass wasn't thought to be wholly impassible, hiking the old abandoned trail, we understood, might prove to be difficult and demanding.[16]

The young Episcopalian minister came, as I recall, from New York, and had little or no experience in hiking mountain trails. But he was eager and vigorous, and he persuaded Father Gallant to undertake a trip. I don't remember how Lew and I came to be invited; maybe Father Gallant wanted a little more company, or he thought our Boy Scout skills might be useful, or we heard about the trip and implored him to take us. Whatever

---

[16] I understand that some years ago it was restored by the Park Service and is now a favorite trail for back-packers, who crowd it during the summer months—a far cry from what it was then.

the reasons, Father invited Lew and me to participate, and we in turn asked our friend Wilfred Goding (another youthful unbeliever!) to join.

The five of us started in Dyea, our backpacks stuffed with blankets and food, and five days later, the food gone, we arrived at Lake Bennett, where we took the train back to Skagway.

I've forgotten some of the details of the trip but I'll never forget our third day out. We spent a brutal eight to ten hours beating our way through maddening barriers of alder and willow, which were interspersed here and there with the sharp, spiky Devil's Club that seemed to reach out to scratch our hands, arms, faces, and clothing. At some points we had to ford and re-ford the headwaters of the Dyea River. If my memory is correct, Father Gallant actually had to pack me across one stretch of rapids on his back. At last, exhausted, we reached the place known as The Scales,[17] because in '97 it was here that the miners had to weigh their supplies to show the Mounties that they were actually taking with them the required thousand or so pounds of supplies needed to see them through the coming months.

Starting out fresh, climbing the Scales would be a breeze for seasoned hikers. Starting out pretty nearly exhausted, as we were, it was formidable. Why didn't we just camp that night at the bottom and start up the next morning? The area at the base was inhospitable, thick with underbrush, without enough flat space for a decent night's sleep, and dense with mosquitoes. So we decided we'd be better off if we climbed to the summit and spent the night there.

Tired as we already were, getting to the top deepened our weariness. We observed that we weren't the first to have found climbing to the Summit under their heavy loads more tiring than they expected. Our predecessors from '97 had left behind their detritus: rusted pick-axes, horse-shoes, iron frying pans, all discarded to lighten their loads; the bones of horses and mules that had died along the way; even an occasional cross that might once have marked the burial place of a gold-seeker who never made it to the summit, let alone to the still-distant Klondike.

---

[17] The ascent that, as I mentioned in Chapter 2, so many people have seen in a photo "of a line of heavily laden men and horses struggling through deep snows at an angle of 30-35 degrees where the trail rises abruptly from the base to the summit of the Pass."

It was nearly midnight when we reached the summit. We found a bare floor open to the sky, the remains of a building, a customs station, perhaps, surviving from '97. Without even cooking supper, we flung ourselves down on the floor fully dressed under a sky that was barely dusk and in a few hours would turn to bright daylight. The floor was as hard as a floor could be. The mosquitoes were terrible.

I slept like a log. I think we all did.

From the Summit our hike was easy: a downhill slope all the way, a day and half to Lake Bennett along lovely ponds, streams, and open forest. The WP&YR regularly stopped at Bennett where in a large wooden building tourists and crew were served lunch. "Hearty lunch" would be an understatement. The kitchen crew soon provided us with a huge meal. Food has never tasted better. An hour or so later, after the train from White Horse had arrived and its load of passengers had eaten their lunch, we got aboard. By mid-afternoon we were home.

Since that day I've hiked and traveled a lot, and yet I remember our hike over the Chilkoot Pass more than seventy years ago as among the most wonderful trips of my life.

❂

There was only one Jewish family in Skagway, no synagogue, and one of the two members of the family was, as best I can tell, only nominally Jewish. Arnold Gutfeld had arrived in Skagway in 1904 at the age of six. His father, Max Gutfeld, must have died before we arrived, and his stepmother, who I presume was Jewish, was something of a recluse and I remember nothing about her.

Her stepson Arnold, however, was active in the community. He worked in the auditor's office of the White Pass and ultimately became auditor; he played on the men's basketball team, the sole competitor of our Skagway High School team; attended the town events, the dances at Elk's Hall in the winter, the Midnight Picnic at Smuggler's Cove on June 20, the annual August picnic at Lake Bennett; and I'm pretty certain that he went to the Presbyterian Church, at least when Griff was the minister. After I had headed off for college he married Frances, who was Irish-American and Roman Catholic. I think their son Arnold was reared as a Catholic.

❂

The result was that like everyone else who grew up in Skagway, by the time I went off to college I had no Jewish friends or acquaintances, and I knew virtually nothing of the American Jewish world or experience. Although I made a few Jewish acquaintances at the University of Washington, I recall no close friends. Because of the conventional bigotry of the time, the fraternity I joined, following the path of Lew and Rod Johnston before me, excluded Jews. It wasn't until my second year in Graduate School when I lived in Washington, D. C., as an intern in the Economics Division of the embattled National Labor Relations Board that, for the first time in my life, I was in the midst of a group of mainly young professionals who were predominantly Jewish, all of them, I think, second generation of Eastern European, mostly Russian, parents, many of whom had fled Russia after the failed 1905 revolution. They were New Yorkers all. For me it was a whole new, fascinating, warm, stimulating, intellectually, culturally, and politically enlightening experience, as it was for another intern, Mary Louise Bartlett, from Providence and Wellesley. Like my growing up in Skagway, that year in Washington decisively shaped my subsequent life, not least in my friendships. But that's another story.

❦

A memory of Skagway during the years long gone when Griff and Father Gallant were both in Skagway came vividly back to me one evening in Rome in 1962. I was there on a year's sabbatical, with Mary, Eric, and Kit. After a dinner on Christmas Eve with some friends from the U.S., we all proceeded to visit several of the major churches in Rome—including one of my favorites, Santa Maria Maggiore—where Midnight Masses were under way. Romans are much more relaxed about their Catholicism than Americans—perhaps because they've lived with the Church for more than a thousand years. That night they flocked into Rome's great churches, whole families and friends, chatting amiably, milling about, and moving on. Here was no solemn Midnight Mass. It was a Roman social event. We followed the Romans' example.

I thought back that night to Skagway. Sometimes on Christmas Eve a fair number of non-Catholics, whether Presbyterians, lapsed Protestants, or non-believers like me, would go to the Catholic church to listen to the choir music and Father Gallant's Latin Mass. The audience was, I remembered, considerably quieter, more respectful, and more austere than in Rome. I've sometimes wondered whether anything like that happened in any other small American towns.

I'd guess not many.

7. The Midnight Sun, 1930

As I've mentioned, Skagway had no newspaper. Although this gap in the town's cultural life stimulated no great outpouring of regret, in the spring of 1930 three Skagway youths decided that they could and would fill that obvious need during the upcoming summer. The three intrepid editors and publishers would be our close friend Rodney Johnston, my brother Lew, and myself. At age 14, I'd just finished my second year in High School; Lew, 15, and Rod, 16, had just finished their junior year.

We thought we could squeeze our newspaper work into our spare time from longshoring on the docks. In that early year of the Great Depression, work was probably going to be slack anyway.

The Midnight Sun would appear once a week, on Saturdays. It was to be eight mimeographed pages, three columns on each page. A cover page would display a scenic sketch, usually of surrounding mountains, by the town's part-time artist, Vic Sparks. Mother, a speedy and accurate typist and a phenomenal speller (she loved crossword puzzles), agreed to type our copy onto the stencils, ordinarily on Friday afternoons and evenings. We hoped to persuade Roger, 8, to run off the stencils on the mimeograph machine (which I believe we borrowed from the school).

We hoped that our fellow townspeople would subscribe—as most of them indeed did. We also thought we might peddle copies to the tourists, who with the stimulus of Vic Sparks' covers, might want to keep them as souvenirs. (As it turned out, that angle never proved to be very successful, even when we printed an entire passenger list to lure them to laying out a dime per copy in order to impress their friends back in Los Angeles or Omaha.) And we could sell advertising space to merchants, hotels, and others.

Catherine Hahn, who was living in Seattle but had grown up in Skagway, where her father V. I. was Superintendent of the WP&YR, agreed to cable us 500 words of news culled from the Friday edition of the Seattle *Times*.

As I mentioned earlier, the cable line, which had been laid down some years earlier by the U. S. Army for military purposes, was Skagway's only means of communication with the Outside. As with telegraph lines, to send a cable you paid by the word. Five hundred words were as much as we could afford.

Catherine performed her task without pay. Her generosity was extraordinary.

When I was stationed at Fort Lewis, Washington, with the 44th Infantry Division, Mary and Ellen, who was barely a year old, came to share what time they could with me during the fall months of 1943. We rented a room in nearby Olympia and whenever I could get a weekend pass I would join them there. Catherine and her husband, it turned out, lived within walking distance, and when Catherine offered us the use of her kitchen for our suppers we gladly accepted. Catherine, a devout Christian Scientist and a practitioner of her church's methods for preventing and overcoming disease, died some years later from cancer.

Here are some excerpts from that summer's editions of *The Midnight Sun*.

From No. 1, June 6, 1930

In this first edition of the MIDNIGHT SUN, we, the editors, wish to sincerely thank [O.K., a split infinitive, so who cared?] those who have so generously contributed to the future support of this paper by subscribing and advertising.

We in turn intend to put forth our best efforts in giving you an interesting and reliable paper.

LANDING FIELD IN PROGRESS. The work on the landing field is progressing rapidly. The stumps have been pulled, old shacks torn down, and it is now being plowed . . . . This is one of the largest fields in Alaska and should stimulate an interest in Skagway in regard to air transportation.

GEO. RAPUZZI LAUNCHES BOAT. George Rapuzzi's new motor-launch, "Teresa" has been in the water a number of days. It is a forty-five foot boat . . . . built to carry about thirty people and will be used to take tourists to all the interesting places on the Lynn Canal.

A dance will be given tonight at the A.B . . . Hall by the Alpine Club to raise funds for the treasury.

BURRO CREEK JOE entertained his first party of excursionists this season on Wednesday and Thursday of last week. Nine ladies went over from Skagway in the "Teresa." Excellent weather permitted outdoor sleeping for those who wished to desert the cabin. The trails were in fine condition and a great deal of hiking was done.

JUNE 14, 1930
SCHMELING WINS ON FOUL IN FOURTH ROUND

New York, June 12: Max Schmeling won the world's Heavy Weight Championship from Jack Sharkey by a foul in the fourth round . . . .

Washington, June 11. Pres. Hoover's law enforcement commission desires the freedom to condemn Prohibition if their findings warrant it . . . .

MRS. L. H. JOHNSTON went as far as Bennett on Wednesday morning.

MR. L. H. JOHNSTON, who has been down river for the past month on C. P. R. business, came in on the train on Wednesday.

JUNE 21, 1930

FIRST DAYS OF '98 DANCE OF SEASON . . . . The [Princess] Alice orchestra furnishing the music. The dance was attended almost wholly by local people, as most of the Alice passengers went on the Taku Arm trip.

FOURTH OF JULY COMMITTEE APPOINTED . . . .

BYRD LANDS AFTER TWENTY MONTHS IN THE ATLANTIC . . . .

Editorial Page

Why is it that the benches on A. B. Mountain have been torn up? . . . .

STANLEY SMITH, who accidentally shot himself in the leg last week, is making satisfactory progress. He was playing with a "22" when the accident happened, which, luckily, was not very serious.

June 28, 1930

HOOVER TO VETO PENSION BILL . . . .

NEW STREET CAR. The Skagway Street Car No. 2 made its first appearance on Thursday. The car was constructed by Mr. Itjen and has occupied most of his spare time during the past winter. It has a capacity for carrying thirty people and makes a very comfortable vehicle for carrying passengers. The artistic lettering and decoration were done by Mr. Wm. Wallace, sr. Miss Charlotte Sparks is conductress.

From 79 degrees Wednesday afternoon to 36 degrees that night is the drop in temperature here, recorded by the government thermometer . . . . *[which happened to be on our back yard, where Dad faithfully recorded the daily changes in temperature.]*

July 6, 1930

MAX SMITH ARRIVES BY PLANE. Mr. Max Smith arrived in Skagway last Saturday night in the Lockheed-Vega plane "Skagway," thus finishing the trip started in Caliente, Mexico on Wednesday of the preceding week. Mr. Smith left Mexico by train on Wednesday. Thursday he flew from Oakland, Cal., to Seattle in a fourteen passenger, tri-moored Fokker. Saturday morning with five other passengers he took off from lake Union in the plane "Skagway" for the various ports en route. Ten hours after leaving Seattle Mr. Smith was in Skagway.

JULY 12, 1930

'MOON ROCKET' SOARS ABOVE EXPECTATIONS. Worcester, Mass., July 9. The Clark University here announced tonight that the experiments of Professor Robert Goddard, with the so called "Moon Rocket," which he had denied was ever intended to reach the moon, gives so much promise of valuable contributions to science that the famous Daniel Guggenheim Fund has made a grant of an unspecified amount, for a continuation or work which has been in progress for fifteen years.

WILBUR STORY returns to Skagway last Sunday after an absence of a year.

A year earlier, Wilbur, an amiable alcoholic who seemed to be acting even more strangely than usual, had been judged by a jury of his peers to be insane and had been sent to the state mental hospital in Morningside, Oregon, where Alaskan residents were assigned when they were duly judged insane (though distinguishing the clinically crazy from the merely eccentric among Skagway residents was by no means easy). From Skagway, it was commonly said, there were only three places to go—Inside (i.e., to the interior of Alaska), Outside (i.e., to what would later be called the Lower Forty-Eight), or Morningside. Wilbur had been sent to Morningside, where he sobered up in due time, and—a fact the editors discreetly omitted—it was from Morningside that he had just returned. In later years Wilbur was fond of remarking that although most people in Skagway would tell you that they were perfectly sane, including some who in Wilbur's view were not, the only person in Skagway who had a piece of paper that actually proved he was sane was himself, Wilbur Story.

MRS. L. H. JOHNSTON and MRS. P. I. DAHL visited in the Simmons home at Carcross this week. They report that the Simmons' mink ranch is a very busy place. It is no small task to take care of 700 mink. It requires 300 pounds of food daily to keep these animals in good condition and this food is cooked in a cooker which holds forty gallons at one time.

Omitted by the editors, possibly at the request of Vera Dahl, who faithfully typed up their reports on the stencils, was the newsworthy fact that throughout their stay in Carcross, Ethel Johnston, Vera Dahl, their hostess, and her daughter played bridge about ten hours a day.

July 26, 1930
JACK DEMPSEY TO BATTLE FOR THE HEAVYWEIGHT TITLE . . .

WARNING! Mayor Mulvihill wishes to warn hikers who walk up the railroad to watch out for "bars" near the third crossing. Six bears, three of them brown and three black, have been sighted there lately and two of these have cubs and are therefore dangerous. Stewart Edward White, the author, says bears are entirely harmless if left alone. All disciples of this writer, therefore, may continue their hiking on the railroad and even play with the cubs and tease the mother if they so desire—or at least they may do so if they are confident they can run just one and a half times as fast as a bear and are able to climb the nearest tree in sight with remarkable rapidity. Otherwise—leave the bears alone, for even bears get hungry at times and occasionally like a nice steak as well as we do. *(Smart-ass editors!)*

Editorial Page
A winter with no hockey seems imminent unless the '98 dances are better patronized . . . .

GEORGE RAPUZZI took a boatload of young folks to Haines last Saturday night to hear the "talkies." *[Seems the "talkies" hadn't yet reached Skagway. And we thought Haines was the backwater.]*

August 2, 1930
BRITISH DIRIGIBLE CROSSES ATLANTIC . . . .

PRINCE FLIES CHANNEL AND LANDS IN BELGIUM . . . .

ENFORCEMENT MEN STRIVE TO SOLVE PROHIBITION PROBLEMS . . . .

SKAGWAY ENJOYS PARADE AND CIRCUS. Skagway witnessed her first parade and a circus on Wednesday evening, when the children of the town formed a line of march at the

Social Center, marching through the principal streets. The parade was led by the "boys band" playing every instrument from cowbells to piccolos. Following the band came "Uncle Sam," "George and Martha Washington," two old fashioned ladies in a coach popular in the days of '98, were next in the process. Their coach was pulled by an unspirited horse resembling Spark Plug, and "Tom Mix" was at the reins. Fierce lions, a tight rope walker, acrobats, flower girls, Hawaiian maidens, a fortuneteller, and the "Bridal Party" followed . . . .

Editorial Page

With the painting of the Standard Oil Buildings and tanks at the dock, Skagway has a sign for airplanes. The workers . . . painted on top of their warehouse the word "Skagway" in large black letters for the benefit of airplanes. This is something every town today needs and Skagway should be proud to have one.

August 9, 1930

MOSCOW HOPEFUL OF U.S. RECOGNITION . . . .

HOOVER INVITED TO SPEAK AT LABOR CONVENTION TO BE HELD IN BOSTON

Last Thursday morning, as Kenneth and Fred Blanchard were hiking over the famous old "Chilkoot Pass . . . they saw a bear ambling toward them and were forced to take to a tree. The episode occurred about one mile north of Finnegan's point, which is about five miles up the Dyea valley. They had seen another bear about one mile before this but that bear did the conventional thing and walked in the other direction. This bruin, however, after being seen by the two Chilkoot hikers, began to walk nonchalantly up to them. Fred and Ken were in no mood to trifle with bears at that moment and so they both slid up a tree. The bear left soon after. On this trip they also saw twenty goats and one moose.

Fred, the elder, later related with considerable amusement that as he and Ken raced madly away looking for a suitable tree to climb, they spotted a skinny birch that might have been just about big enough for one person. At that instant Ken shouted: "Fred! Here's my tree! Where's yours?"

After surviving the bear scare, Fred went on to earn his Ph.D. at Columbia, and four years later we learn from The Midnight Sun of June 23, 1934:

MR. AND MRS. W.G. BLANCHARD of this city received word that their son Fred is now a proud father, his wife having given birth to a baby daughter on June 11. The daughter, who has been named Barbara Ann, was born in Moscow, Idaho, where Fred is head of the Dept. of Dramatic Art at the University of Idaho.

I'll bet he was never involved in a more dramatic performance than the one in Dyea, where he and Ken performed their one act drama with no audience except the grizzly.

FIFTEEN THOUSAND PASSED THROUGH HERE IN AUGUST 1897. Mrs. Carl Larson is the owner of an old paper of August '97 telling of the rush of people to the North. On August 22nd, 1897, just 33 years ago, there was a total of 31 vessels on their way for the Klondike regions, in the yet unexplored, and vastly unknown section of the world--the extreme north. These 31 ships, which were sailing from the western ports of San Francisco and Seattle, carried a total of 15,592 passengers for the Klondike . . . .

MRS. F. J. VAN DE WALL entertained a group of intimate friends and neighbors of Mrs. M. Conway on Friday evening. The affair was a surprise to the guest of honor. Sewing was the diversion of the evening, at the close of which the hostess served a delicious luncheon. *[O.K., luncheon at night. So you want to make something of it?]*

AUGUST 30, 1930

Editorial Page

THANK YOU. This issue, no. 13, of the Midnight Sun, will be the last one published by the editors this season . . . .

With the end of August here, we again see the closing of the tourist season . . . . Some summers are good and some are no so good. Although this past summer may have been one of the latter, we must remember that "there's a silver lining in every cloud" and there is always another summer coming.

8. A Walk Up Broadway

When I look beyond the fine detail to the coarse grained picture, I see Skagway as probably the most egalitarian place I've ever known. (Here again, of course, I refer only to the white population.) In that respect, Skagway may not have been all that different from many other western or Midwestern small towns.

The people who settled there brought little social baggage along. One's "family" in Skagway was just that: one's family in Skagway, nothing more. Anyone who had tried to hoist the family coat of arms in that town, assuming anyone could claim any family origins to brag about, which maybe nobody did, would soon have lowered it to escape the hoots of laughter. Not that your family was unimportant. But as I said, the only family members who counted for anything were the ones who lived right there in Skagway or, like my Grandma Lewis, were frequent enough visitors to be known to some of the residents.

I've sometimes wondered what a visiting sociologist in search of class and status would have made of Skagway as it was then. To recapture the reality of that time and place, it would help enormously to have recorded interviews with the entire population of Skagway in 1930 or so. After all, 500 subjects isn't an excessive number for a diligent social scientist to interview, especially one with a nice research budget and a few assistants. Regrettably (perhaps) no social scientist ever studied Skagway.

I can easily guess, though, what he—in those days it probably would have been a male—might have observed.

Suppose we walk around the town with our imaginary visitor.

Maybe the first thing our sociologist discovers, nosing around for differences in status and class, is that in Skagway the term status is never used and class means, well, just a class in school or maybe in college. Yet our sociologist still might find something—not a lot, but something—by asking two simple questions: who works where at what, and what difference does it make?

Broadway

During my years in Skagway the single set of narrow gauge rails of the White Pass Railroad run smack down the length of Broadway. Placing them there originally was just practical. Now their location is also nicely symbolical.

Skagway in the 1920s and '30s is a one-company town, completely dependent on one major employer and one reason for existence: the railroad.[18] As a town occupied by white newcomers, Skagway came into existence because of its location, and that reason doesn't change in my time there. Passenger ships, freighters, tankers, and coal ships from Vancouver and Seattle bring tourists and freight to the northernmost end of the Inland Passage: Skagway. Many of the summer tourists go by train on up to Lake Bennett and back, or perhaps they travel on to Carcross for a trip on a riverboat to nearby Lake Lindeman, or even to the railroad's northern terminus at Whitehorse. Maybe some go even further down the Yukon River on a paddle-wheel steamer—owned and operated, naturally, by the White Pass and Yukon Route Railway Company. On the return trip back down to Skagway from Whitehorse, Carcross, and Bennett, the WP&YR

---

[18] It would be many decades, remember, before a highway is cut through the mountains to Whitehorse.

carries passengers and sometimes hauls open gondolas packed with sacks of silver-lead ore from the Yukon interior. At Skagway, freight and passengers are loaded on to the awaiting passenger ships or freighters for the trip back down the Inland Passage to Vancouver and Seattle.

With boats coming in three or four times a week and trains running daily, from June to Labor Day Skagway is a busy, bustling place. In early September the bustle abruptly stops. By mid-September or thereabouts, the boats are coming in only once every two weeks, and the trains to Whitehorse are down to two or three a week. For the next nine months, Skagway is a quiet town. A lot of us actually like it that way.

Yet even in winter the railroad line has to be kept open. That means work for the crews who man the snowplows, which are mounted on the locomotives at the Railroad Shops way up at the North End of town. During Christmas vacation I sometimes go to Whitehorse with Lew and Wil Goding, whose dad, a locomotive engineer, shares a cabin in Whitehorse with one or two other trainmen. From the Summit onward, when I look out the train windows I see nothing but a wall of snow, so high that we seem to be traveling through a snow-packed tunnel, which sometimes we really are.

❦

A sociologist is professionally predisposed to look for the differences between white collars and blue collars. If he begins with the white collars, a walk along Broadway will tell him some of what he's looking for.

Broadway ends just a few hundred yards from the high tide line on the Bay that marks the southernmost end of the town. At that bottom of Broadway you are just a few steps away from the barn-red building that houses the White Pass headquarters, where you can also buy your railroad tickets. At the moment our sociologist is more interested in checking out the small white-collar staff.

Among them is the General Manager, George Miller, the highest ranking railroad official in the town, who is appointed by and responsible to the British board of directors. George Miller, a Canadian, remains in Skagway during the summer, and winters at the company headquarters in Vancouver. Dad and Mother think highly of George Miller. In 1929 when my brother Lew, the town's only Eagle Scout, is unable to attend the International Boy

Scout Jamboree in Britain because of the cost, an anonymous donor provides the funds. My parents are confident that the donor is George Miller.

For all practical purposes the person directly in charge of the White Pass is not Mr., Miller, however, but the Superintendent, V. I. (for Victor Imanuel) Hahn. V. I., as he is generally called (though, except by a few people like Dad, not to his face) came from Pennsylvania, where he was educated as a mechanical engineer. He and his wife are in some way assumed, I suppose, to be at the top of the social pinnacle. Although on rare occasions Dad, Mother, and we boys are invited for dinner, V. I. and his wife aren't among Dad and Mother's close friends. (I'm not sure who is, and some years later, looking back, I'll wonder whether maybe they weren't a bit lonely.)

The Auditor is a hard-drinking Scot, Alec Blanchard, who with his petite and pretty wife Olive are a part of one of the social circles to which Mother and Dad belong.

A photo taken in 1939 shows the fourteen men then working in the White Pass Office. Among them are V. I. and his son Carl; Alec Blanchard and his son Alec, Jr. (I knew him as Bud); Ken Hannan, from Jamaica, the husband of Mother's much loved friend Dusty, from England; Louis Selmer, the son of Oscar, the town barber; and Arnold Gutfeld.

What none of the smiling men in the photo know is that Alec Senior will die during the next decade. His wife Olive will move to a cabin in Dyea to share a hermit's life with the ghost town's only resident. Bud Blanchard, a handsome young man who displays a dazzling smile in the photo, will follow his dad along the path of heavy drinking, at least for a while. George Miller, after his retirement a few years later, will end up penniless during the Great Depression; supposedly he is once seen by someone from Skagway begging on the streets of Vancouver. Sic transit . . .

Ken Hannan will in time succeed to the post of General Manager. Several years after the photo is taken, his wife Dusty, Mother's dear friend, will die in Seattle. Louis Selmer will die at 50. His wife Alice (Story), with whom I was infatuated during my senior year in high school before she wisely cashed me in for Louis, will re-marry—to Bob Selmer, Louis' younger brother and a life-long friend of my brother Roger.

Arnold Gutfeld, the town's one nominal Jewish male, will marry a Roman Catholic schoolteacher—she will be Roger's teacher in the third grade—and will succeed Alec Blanchard as auditor.

It's a small town.

❦

If our sociologist leaves the White Pass office and walks north on Broadway, he'll surely be struck by the large number of wooden buildings, mostly one-story, maybe two at most, all with the squared-off second story façade that we have seen in every cowboy movie filmed in a Hollywood version of a Western town. A fair number of them, now weather worn and run down, are visibly empty and evidently have been empty for years. Interspersed among these relics of Skagway's flourishing past are the stores that serve the people of Skagway year around and maybe the tourists during the summer. Here's a sample.

Just up Broadway is Richter's jewelry store. In 1897 at the age of seven Emil Richter arrived in Skagway with his parents from Tacoma, Washington. He went to work for Perry Hern, who owned the store that Emil eventually bought from him and renamed Richter's. Emil now makes gold nugget jewelry, silver spoons, knives, ashtrays and other items that appeal to the summer tourist trade; when business tapers off in the fall and winter he repairs watches, clocks, and other delicate mechanisms. His eldest son Ed is one of my classmates and will be one of the six who graduate with me in 1932. Claire, the younger, often plays guard next to me on our high school basketball team. Like their mother, Ed works in the store during the busy season. After his dad dies and his mother leaves for Seattle, Ed will buy the store from her.

Up Broadway and across the street is the Washington Fruit Store, which everyone calls Rapuzzi's because it is owned by Ma Rapuzzi, the Genoese matriarch of one of Skagway's most respected and hardworking families. Her son Charlie is a White Pass locomotive engineer. Son George has worked his way up from messenger boy to top-flight machinist at the railroad shops. George is a formidable practical joker, as I'll describe later, and a dedicated collector of memorabilia, from abandoned car motors to an old roulette table. In later years he'll deposit his huge collection of "antiques" in several warehouses that he turns into a museum. Daughter Della is secretary to the General Manager of the White Pass. In the 1930s, son Louis becomes United States Marshall, in which role he plays a small part in the Dahl saga known in our family as "When the crazy man chased Dad down Broadway." (I'll save that story for a later chapter.)

In Mother's reminiscences on her 90th birthday she recalled, correctly, I presume, that because Ma Rapuzzi couldn't write in English, to keep track of sales she relied on her infallible memory until Della came home from work, when, as Mother put it,

"Ma would say to Della, 'Look at page so-and-so. Mrs. So-and-so bought groceries today, and I know she didn't put it all down.' We all had our page, you know, and charged it and then paid at the end of the month."

The biggest building on Broadway is the hotel where we stayed a few nights after our arrival. The Golden North Hotel is run by George Dedman's widow, Clara, and their son Henry Alaska. Clara, one of the old-timers, was born in Oregon in 1861 and arrived in Skagway in 1898. (In 1936, the year of Clara's death, the hotel would be taken over by the owners of the house in which we first lived in Skagway, the Tropea family—another sign of how lives intersect in a small town!)

Next door to the Golden North is Dedman's Photo Shop run by Henry's wife Bessie.

The photo shop, which continues to operate under the ownership of their daughter Barbara, is today a veritable museum, with an extraordinary collection of photos dating back to the Gold Rush days.

Still further along Broadway is Ask's Store, owned and operated by Harry Ask, who arrived from Seattle at the age of five and has created Skagway's biggest grocery and dry goods store. During the three summers of *The Midnight Sun*, Harry Ask is our best advertiser, regularly buying a half column on the last page (though I think we actually write the ads after finding out from Harry what he wants to emphasize.) Here is the text of several.

JULY 5, 1930

Read These! Girls Triangle Scarfs Silk Crepe $1.50—More Dresses Some With Panties $2.50—Silk Pongee—C. W. Ask and Son.

AUGUST 2, 1930

Hiking and Hunting Outfits. Black Bear Water Repellent Lace Breeches are light, long-wearing and waterproof. $5.70—Black Bear Hunting Coats and Stag overshirts to match the breeches at $6.15 and up—Soft, suede leather

Jackets will turn wind and rain and wear for years, Sizes 36-46, $14.75—Ladies suede finish Gloves, $1.25—Fresh Haines strawberries today—C. W. Ask and Son.

August 18, 1934

NEW! Brocade paper Napkins. Large pkgs. 35¢ Birthday cards 5 10 15¢—We now have full information on the 1935 Philco radios priced from $21.00 and up. 49 models to CHOOSE from.—JELLO ICE CREAM Powder Vanilla, Chocolate and Lemon Flavors. 2 pkgs. 25¢—Last Call on CANNING Peaches & Prunes $1.15 per crate. H. G. ASK

September 17, 1935

To YOU & YOU & YOU. In this last issue, we wish to thank you for your liberal Patronage and response to our ads. For your kind consideration of any errors due to the difficulties of conducting two places of business.—Everything will be under one roof by Oct. 1, when we open one of the most modern & sanitary meat shops to be had. May we hope for a continuation of your patronage? We will show our appreciation by giving you the best we can in service and prices. CONSIDER THIS YOUR STORE. H. G. ASK.

❦

If Harry knew, he chose not to reveal his observation that when I was a slightly delinquent eleven, maybe twelve, along with a couple of my buddies—Mark Lee?, Bud Blanchard?—on several occasions I sneaked candy bars and cigarettes off his shelves. My fellow delinquents and I hiked up the trail to Lower Lake, stopping along the way to eat our stolen candy and smoke our stolen cigarettes, leaving behind a trail of cigarette butts and candy wrappers (shame! shame!) that revealed our delinquency to anyone who might be coming close behind. On one occasion, a man from the town—I've forgotten who it was—happened to overtake us. "You've left quite a trail, boys," he said. "I know what you're up to." Whether because of that experience or for other reasons, I soon started to resist the lure of petty crime—except maybe for an occasional effort, sometimes successful, to hit a street light with a well-aimed stone—and entered upon the Path of Righteousness, more or less. Well, there was one exception. When I was about fifteen an attempt to steal a heaving line from a tourist boat ended so disastrously that it forever scared me away from the temptations of thievery. Of that episode, more later.

❁

On the other side of Broadway there is a large, old, rather run-down building that houses Harrison's Dry Goods and Hardware Store. It is owned by a widow lady, who as lonely widows and widowers have been known to do, evidently welcomes the company of someone (as we say in these politically backward times) of the opposite sex. Among these, or for all I know her sole occasional companion, is Mr. Tanner, a good and decent man and respected member of our community.

Here is Mother's account:

"Well, about midnight, a young man about town came to the door for Doctor, and told him he was needed down at [the widow's] apartment . . . . She had a boyfriend, who was a widower. It was Mr. Tanner. And he had passed out, died, having intercourse. And later, his daughter came up, of course, for the funeral and everything, and Doctor was there and heard her. She said to this woman, "I hope you burn in hell." And you know, she did burn to death. Her store caught fire, and she went back [into the store]. She had some lovely jewelry, and she went back to get it and [the fire] caught her."

❁

A little further on we come to one of the most important social centers in Skagway—Selmer's Barber Shop. Oscar Selmer, Sr., the barber, was born in Oslo around 1880, as was his wife, Paula. Both arrived in Skagway in 1905, where they have raised (no one in Skagway says "reared") a family of five sons and two daughters—all active in school, sports, work.

❁

One of the daughters, Pauline, will be one of the six members of my 1932 graduating class in high school. Many years later, Oscar, Junior, will grow a long beard and serve several terms on the town council. Louis, one of the town's best athletes, will marry my classmate Alice Story and die at the age of forty-one. Alice will re-marry Louis younger brother Bob, who, years later after they have moved to Seattle, will become a golfing partner of Roger's. At the annual Skagway reunion in Seattle in May 2000, while chatting with Alice I say that during our senior year I was quite infatuated with her. She looks a bit surprised, and says, "You should have spoken up!"

After The Gold Rush   57

❁

Like just about everyone else in town, I get my hair cut at Selmer's. Dad often goes there for a shave as well—yes, "a shave and a haircut, six bits." More important, not many days go by when he doesn't drop in to Selmer's Barber Shop to get caught up on the local news. "Local news" is what the men call it. When women get together to catch up on the local news, the men call it "gossip." But real men don't gossip. They just catch up on the news.

Oscar was also a talented musician, and I have a faded memory of his performing in black face at the Elk's lodge in a minstrel show, playing a violin. *(I know. In those days we didn't realize—or ignored—the implications that would be perceived in a minstrel show in a more enlightened time.)*

❁

From Selmer's Barber Shop we proceed almost to the end of the Broadway business area. There in all its grandeur stands the only poured-concrete structure in town, the Alaska National Bank. Jack Conway, ten years my senior, later recalled that when it was built in 1916, "most of us had never seen a concrete building, much less see one being constructed. Many days after school, we kids would come down to the site and watch in fascination as Bob Lee dug out the foundation with a team of horses and a scraper."[19]

The Alaska National Bank is owned and run by Mr. Rasmussen, who retains a trace of his Swedish accent. Mr. Rasmussen is not, as I remember, a highly popular man in Skagway; but perhaps small town bankers rarely are. On the other hand, his son Elmer, who went out to college and on to Harvard Business School and now works in the bank for his father, is popular with some of us younger kids for whom he has served as our Scoutmaster.

Some years later, after a branch of the Bank is established in Anchorage, Elmer will take over its ownership and operation, and as branches of the Bank expand throughout the Territory and later the State, Elmer will become one of the wealthiest men in Alaska, and also the most generous donor to charitable causes in that State. His sister Evangeline, whom I barely knew, will also move to Anchorage, where, as the wife of the publisher of the Anchorage Times, *Alaska's leading newspaper, she will prove to*

---

[19] His recollections are in Carl Nord's documents.

be perhaps the city's leading social figure. That, at any rate, was my impression in 1987 when I received an honorary degree from the University of Alaska in Anchorage.

What we call "Downtown" ends on Broadway at the Post Office, a part of that same poured concrete building, a few feet up the street from the Bank. The U.S. Postmaster, Martin Conway, was born in Ireland in 1876 and arrived in Skagway from Seattle in 1898, which makes him one of the old-timers. A staunch Democrat, he was appointed to his post under the Wilson Administration in 1913 and during the few years after we arrived and before he died in 1930, Dad often stops by the Post Office on his way down from the Hospital not only to pick up our mail, if any, but, more important, to chat with a fellow Democrat about the iniquities of Herbert Hoover and the Republicans. Sadly, Martin Conway will not live to see a second great Democrat defeat the detested Hoover and gain the presidency in the elections of 1932. In the interval, though, he and Dad can enjoy their partisan jibes, indifferent to or even spurred on by the presence of any putative Republican who happens to be picking up mail.

Martin Conway will be succeeded by Henley Murray, a native born Skagwayite (though in Skagway parlance not a "native," a term reserved for Indians, or, today, Native-Americans.) This is lucky for Dad, because Henley Murray is appointed by FDR in 1933, and is, I assume, also a fellow Democrat. So the partisan chats will continue.

Let's leave the Bank and P.O. behind us and amble North on the wooden sidewalk. For the next half dozen blocks Broadway is lined with houses, most of them lived in, a few abandoned, and an occasional open lot. The houses are all built of wood, one or two stories high, painted in various colors from white to red and blue, adequately maintained, surrounded by grass, shrubs, flowers, perhaps a vegetable garden in back. These places probably wouldn't look out of place in many a western or midwestern town.

Glancing westward at 11th Avenue we see the school—Skagway Public School, two stories, all twelve grades. I'll say more about school later. Meanwhile, not far along we see the hospital—the WP&YR hospital where Dad carries on his practice with two or three nurses, all employees of the Railroad. For such a small town, the hospital building is huge, a bit ramshackle-looking, as if it was originally built for some other purposes—hotel, warehouse—if I ever knew I no longer remember.

The Hospital

Inside it is clean, neat, tidy. Dad's small office is on the first floor. Nearby is his ancient x-ray machine, which, he learns too late, shoots its radiation around like a leaky hose. Some years later Dad will discover a persistent growth on his right hand. It's cancer, of course, and he will end up missing a finger.

Because of the town's relative isolation, Dad is compelled to deal with emergencies that no general practitioner in an urban setting in the Lower Forty-Eight would have to assume. Even in the summer months, a patient lucky enough to take a boat out the next day wouldn't arrive in Seattle in less than five days; in the winter, the patient might have to wait two weeks for the ship to come in, and another five days to reach Seattle.

In later years, I would often try to imagine the cases he had to take on that in other circumstances he would have referred to a specialist or a hospital emergency room. He must have coped well, somehow, because those who lived in Skagway during his years there all seem to have felt confidence in him and great affection, which they never failed to express to me when I met them in later years. I'll say more about Dad's life in Skagway (and Mother's) in a later chapter.

Perhaps the good memories Dad left behind in Skagway were reinforced by the absence of a successor. A few years after Dad and Mother left Skagway in 1950, the railroad, fallen on hard times, dropped its support for the hospital and its staff. The building was torn down, to be replaced in time by "The Dahl Memorial Clinic," which has a visiting nurse. Nowadays, anyone needing medical care beyond the capabilities of the nurse can fly the next day to Juneau, Anchorage, or Seattle.

Although we could continue our walk and end up at that bustling center of maintenance and repair, the railroad shops—known to Skagway residents simply as "the Shops"—let's head back down toward the residential areas where most Skagwayites made their homes.

But first, a pause to read *The Midnight Sun.*

9. The Midnight Sun, 1934

Lew, now 19, had just returned from his junior year at the University of Washington; I'm 18 and I'd just finished my sophomore year there. Rod had concluded that, despite its exceptional quality, *The Midnight Sun* just couldn't make enough money to make it worth his time. Maybe if we split the profits two ways—what profits?—Lew and I might come out a little ahead by the end of the summer. This year we published on both Saturday and Wednesday.

From June 23, 1934

PRESIDENT ROOSEVELT MAINTAINS POPULARITY . . . .

SEATTLE STRIKERS INJURED IN STRIFE WITH POLICE . . . .

Editorial Page

VOLUME TWO, NUMBER ONE OF THE MIDNIGHT SUN IS OFFERED TO YOU TODAY with some doubts, not without a few misgivings, but nonetheless with hope for the future. This issue has mistakes, many of them; however, we want to ask you to bear with us a while longer, for we have been rushed as to time—but we did want to get started as soon as possible . . . .

We intend to write editorials . . . and when we write them that means that we two, at least, believe that they are right. That doesn't mean they are right. That doesn't make them right at all, and some will differ from us. That is just as it should be and is expected. But, in connection with this we wish to emphasize that what we write is written by us alone, not our parents nor by our friends, and criticisms should in no case be directed at them.

We're in a rather tough spot in regard to editorials, because there are some things we can't write and other things of which we are not supposed to write. [What these forbidden topics were I no longer remember, but probably something bearing on the WP&YR. Or was it gossip about who may have been fornicating with whom? Hey, hadn't we heard about the First Amendment? Yes, but . . .] In consequence, when we do write an article, we have had to survey it from several angles, so if you don't always agree with what we offer, at least recall what we've said here.

This paper isn't going to be a metropolitan daily. [Surprise, surprise!] . . . . This paper is for Skagway and surrounding territory—we hope—and it will be written in our own style—far cry though that may be from what is good journalism.

After all that palaver, I wonder who would read the paper. Maybe no one did. Maybe they just subscribed and saved it for starting fires in the winter. Well, there were always the personal notices . . .

CONGRATULATIONS, HAROLD! Word was received here recently that Harold Hestness, recently graduated by the University of Washington Law School, had been made a member of the Order of the Coif, the highest honor awarded by the University Law School . . . Harold had previously made an excellent record at the University, where he made a lightweight crew letter, was made a member of Varsity Boat Club, Oval Club (one of the highest activity honoraries on the campus), and Delta Theta Phi (national law professional) and still had time to make a great number of friends. The Midnight Sun and Skagway are proud of, and extend congratulations to Harold.

*Harold was also a charter member of the WALKA group—W, A, L, K, A:. **W**ilfred Goding, Harold **A**. Hestness, Rodney **L**ewis Johnston, Lewis **K**itchener Dahl, and Robert **A**lan Dahl. WALKA was the name five good friends chose for the boat we all owned together. Harold was the son of a brakeman who had been killed in a railroad accident. Although the White Pass may have provided the family some compensation, Harold felt it was inadequate and bore a fierce anger toward the railroad management. Perhaps as a result, he became a radical of sorts, and remained so, I think, even after a highly successful career in Seattle real estate had made him a wealthy man.*

From June 30, 1934

MAHATMA GANDHI ESCAPES ATTEMPT ON LIFE . . . .

ROOSEVELT OVER-THROWS TRADITION, VETOES BILLS . . .

MAYOR MULVIHILL EXTENDS WARNING. Mayor Mulvihill requests that parents caution their children not use the airfield for a playground nor cross the field going to or coming from the "old swimming hole." *[This was a spring-fed creek where the water was only slightly warmer than the Bay. Maybe a few kids learned to swim there. I never did.]* . . . . One pilot this week had to take to the air again to avoid what might have been a very serious accident.

Advertisements

For Wedding Gifts
Bridge Prizes, etc.
Framed Alaska views
DEDMAN'S PHOTO SHOP

F.O. EAGLES #25
Next Meeting
July 18
Harry Tonkin, W.P.
L.C. Gault, Secy.

While you're in
Skagway—stop at
THE
GOLDEN NORTH HOTEL

WHITE PASS LODGE #113
F & A. M.
July 14 at 8 P. M.

Eat at the
SKAGWAY COFFEE SHOP
Good wholesome meals
Phone 33

ST. MARK'S CATHOLIC
CHURCH
7 A.M. High Mass,
Sermon and Benediction at
Church
No Evening Devotions
Rev. G. E. Gallant,
Pastor

THE PULLEN HOUS
Best in the North
Try it!
Mrs. Harriet Pullen
Proprietress

TOURIST CAFÉ
Breakfast   40¢
Merchants Lunch   35¢
Regular Dinner   40¢
Sunday Dinner   50¢

FIRST PRESBYTERIAN CHURCH
Morning Worship
At 11 A.M.
Sunday School
at 12:15
Warren Griffiths,
Pastor

James Cagney-Ruby
Keeler-Dick Powell
In FOOTLIGHT PARADE
Saturday and Sunday
BROADWAY THEATRE

DR. C.L. POLLEY
Skagway
Dentist
Office and Residence
in Ward Apartments

VISIT
The ALASKA ART
STORE
Original Oil and
Water Color
Paintings
-by-
V.L. SPARKS
Skagway on Broadway
Next to the
Tea Room

From June 27, 1934

TRI-MOTORED PLANE ARRIVES IN SKAGWAY. Four hours and thirty-five minutes to make the trip from Hazelton, B.C., to Skagway is the time it took the new tri-motored all metal Ford plane which arrived last Monday afternoon . . . .

TOURIST SEASON OPENS AS LINES ADD NEW BOATS. Skagway's annual tourist season was unofficially begun last Wednesday morning by the arrival of the Princess Louise with one hundred forty passengers, one hundred of whom were round trippers . . . .

NO CABLE NEWS THIS ISSUE. As you have already undoubtedly noticed, we have no cable news this issue, our policy being to print that only in our Saturday edition. Such a policy is determined, not by our desire to please our readers, but by expediency; for we find that with the bare margin on which we must work it would be impossible to pay for cable news twice a week and still keep out of the red . . . .

Editorial Page

THOUGHTS OF A BACKWOODS PHILOSOPHER. Note: this column, which will be published from time to time, must not be construed as a statement of the editorial policy of this paper, but only as an attempt to set forth one interpretation of certain contemporary problems.

Where people are educated and have attempted to analyze calmly the various political problems—among the intelligentsia, so to speak—one finds that one's political beliefs are accepted complacently.

. . . As we travel away from these "intellectual centers" we find that this attitude changes. It becomes constantly more difficult to engage in an intelligent attempt to find an answer to these apparently unanswerable problems . . . .

The writer rants on and on in this vein.

I am obliged to confess that I was the Backwoods Philosopher. This youthful editor comes across to me now as a rather intellectually arrogant and patronizing young man who, having just finished his sophomore year at the University of Washington, reveals here his . . . well, sophomoric attitudes.

My exposure to the nose-to-nose combat favored by left wing intellectuals in the 1930s and later, was still to come.

That I remained on good terms with my fellow Skagwayites testifies either to their habitual tolerance of one of their "own boys"— "Oh, that's just Bob sounding off"—or, more likely, to not having read beyond the first paragraph.

From July 4, 1934

BROOKS, SKAGWAY OLDTIMER, RETURNS. "I first arrived in Skagway on July 12, 1897 with fifteen mules. The mules were pushed off the boat and swam ashore. I was later put off the boat myself, and made my camp on the beach," thus related J.H. Brooks, one of the most famous of the old packers, here yesterday. Brooks, who is making his first trip to Alaska since 1905, is accompanied by Charles L. Roberts, his business manager and partner, and Allan Menefee, collaborator.

He is returning to his old stamping grounds after almost thirty years to collect data for a forthcoming book of his thrilling experiences . . . . He and a man by the name of Turner first blazed out the famed Chilkoot Pass, or Trail of 97, and he was the first to take a mule over it. "I carried over the goods of the Northwest Mounted Police at a fabulous price, often making as much as $5,000 daily from all my packings," he said. His seventeen mules eventually increased to 335; he had his corrals in the territory now covered by the aviation field . . . .

(Joe Brooks would die on the Trail in 1935).

Editorial Page

TO US, THE GIVING OF CASH PRIZES IN THE SPORTING EVENTS ON THE FOURTH OF JULY REPRESENTS AT BEST A WHOLLY UNNECESSARY EVIL. Ever since we have been old enough to do so we ourselves have constantly participated in sports, and the question which, of late, we have frequently asked ourselves, has been, "What is the value of sport?" We believe that the prime value of sports is a fourfold one. In the first place . . . by . . . keeping one's body in good condition, it puts one in a frame of mind which helps to make life worth living. Again, . . . we . . . gain many valuable and lifelong friendships. Moreover, it gives one a sense of self-confidence . . . . And finally, it teaches one life itself. It teaches one to have contempt for the man who doesn't go in to win, but it also teaches one to have contempt for the person who goes in solely to win.

The sermon goes on for another column. Did Lew write it, or I? It could have been either of us. I have to admit, though, that among the things I recall with pleasure about the Fourth of July in Skagway was winning contests and spending some of my prize money on a once-a-year banana-split-with-vanilla ice cream at Keller's Drug Store.

"SOMEONE IN SKAGWAY HAS BEEN SHOT!" We've never heard these dire words here . . . But some day we're going to . . . . The last few years both the men and boys of Skagway have been using firearms in a manner indicative of either no knowledge or no thought—likely the latter . . . . But unless we all, not just a few, start knowing exactly what we're shooting, knowing that our bullets can't possibly travel a sickening path of death . . . someday we'll hear a mother sadly say, "No, Jack isn't with us any more. He was accidentally killed last year."

IAN MURRAY, vacationing at Big Salmon, saw a bear while out walking with Mr. Hayes, telegraph operator, and his son. The bear proved to be one of the biggest grizzlies Mr. Hayes has yet seen.

From July 7, 1934
FRANCE DENIES CONSPIRACY IN GERMAN UPRISING

WASHINGTON DEMANDS INTEREST ON GERMAN WAR DEBT

Editorial Page

. . . . For the past several years just at a time when the coveys of young grouse were still helpless and comparatively tame, . . . several men and boys . . . have . . . ruthlessly slaughtered them . . . If the young ones are killed, a whole mating season is gone for naught; the birds are scarcely edible and there is no means for the increased propagation of the species . . . . In this way sportsmen who do wait until Sept. 1st are robbed of practically any chance of obtaining the full grown birds . . . .

Notice, dear reader, that the editors aren't against hunting grouse. They just want to make sure that enough adult grouse will be around when the hunting season opens each September.

WE WISH TO apologize if what we laughingly call our newspaper seems somewhat worse than usual. One half the editing and publishing staff is on a strike for several days. Playing baseball on the Fourth, he pushed a finger out of joint on his right hand. As a result, he is a total dern loss as far as the other half of the paper is concerned. More so than usual. If possible!

S.S. HALEAKALA MAKES FIRST ALASKA TRIP . . . . The liner, which was built in 1923, is 360 feet long . . . . Its luxurious appointments will accommodate 326 passengers. The Alaska Steamship Company has extended a special invitation to Skagway people to visit the boat while it is in port next Wednesday.

Advertisement: Our Line of Staple and Fancy Groceries is still quite complete. Let us have your orders. With the arrival of the Haleakala next week we will have our large stock back to normal. SPECIAL SATURDAY 10½ lb. Sugar for 60¢ Limit 10½ lb. to a customer. HARRY G. ASK.

MR. GEDNEY, of Squaw Creek, was in Skagway for the Fourth of July celebration.

When he probably became staggering drunk. More later of the tragic life of Ed Gedney.

FROM JULY 11, 1934

EDITORIAL PAGE

IT WAS SUGGESTED TO US THE OTHER DAY THAT WE STOP OUR EDITORIAL CRITICIZING LONG ENOUGH TO DO SOME BOOSTING. In surprise we looked over our past editorials . . . and we discovered that every one was a criticism. This disconcerts us considerably. For we are essentially praisers, not critics, of Alaska and Skagway. When we are away from home we are constantly on the alert to defend this country of ours [i.e. Alaska] from criticism. Yet when we return home . . . all our editorials are criticisms. What, we wondered, is the explanation for this phenomenon? . . . The primary reason lies in the difficulty of writing praises without sounding like a schoolboy orator . . . . Moreover, we accept the good things rather complacently . . . . So you may now expect us to take an issue one of these days and do some boosting.

Well, maybe. But THOUGHTS OF A BACKWOODS PHILOSOPHER follows in the adjacent column, and he still sounds to me less like Plato or Aristotle than like a Backwoods Preacher desperately trying to rescue his flock from their cardinal sins—political sins, of course.

FROM JULY 14, 1934

EDITORIAL PAGE

. . . . [W]e feel that this is an opportune time to propose something . . . to do with fishing in the two Dewey Lakes . . . When men working on the boats which come in here go up and bring down half a sack full [of trout] . . . there is but one result . . . . In almost any other place where fishing is common in fresh waters, there are regulations regarding the maximum number and the minimum size. And that is what we propose here. We think that ten fish a person is enough, and that anything under six inches should be returned to the water . . . .

H. WHEELER MAKES INTERESTING TRIP TO DAWSON. Mr. H. Wheeler and Pilot Verne Bookwalter left Skagway last Sunday morning at 11:20 for a very interesting trip to Dawson and back. They arrived at Whitehorse one hour later [n. b., 110 miles north], and left there at 2:50 that afternoon for Dawson, [300 miles from Whitehorse] which they reached at 6:30 . . . . They stopped, during the course of their flight to and from Dawson, at several lakes normally not haunted by human beings, and reported that large numbers of caribou abounded there.

Verne Bookwalter was among the first transcontinental U.S. Airmail pilots, after which he became one of Alaska's first and finest "bush pilots," flying a pontoon plane to remote lakes, rivers, and inlets. His wife became one of Mother's close friends.

CARIBOU HERDS THRILL TOURISTS ON YUKON . . . . [M]any tourists have been thrilled by the herds of swimming caribou which were seen on the last few trips of the steamers down the Yukon . . . . [T]he crew of the Steamer Casca saw a herd of caribou . . . which they estimated to be made up of 200 or more. The passengers from the Steamer Yukon also reported that they saw literally thousands of caribou on the last trip.

FROM JULY 25, 1934

EDITORIAL PAGE

MANY GREAT THINGS ARE CONCEIVED AND BORN IN THE REALMS OF CIGAR SMOKE AND HOT AIR BUT MOST OF THEM DIE THERE ALSO . . . . And that is where our potential swimming pool lies gasping for breath right now . . . . IF WE ARE TO HAVE A POOL THIS SUMMER, WE MUST HAVE TWO THINGS: ACTION AND LEADERSHIP.

GRIFFITHS AND DAHL WIN IN HARD FOUGHT TENNIS MATCH. With the ball becoming a fast grey shadow, Warren Griffiths and Doc Dahl [i.e., Lew] downed Louis and Vic Selmer last night in three sets of good, hard racking tennis, and in so doing ushered in the new tennis tournament . . . .

70   THE MIDNIGHT SUN, 1934

ROD JOHNSTON AND JOE McCANN hiked to the peak of Dome Mountain yesterday and reported that the scenery they saw en route was very beautiful.

ADVERTISEMENTS

WE HAVE JUST RECEIVED A HUNDRED CASES OF HOP GOLD BEER. WE STILL HAVE ON HAND ALL OTHER POPULAR BRANDS AND MIXTURES. ALL BRANDS CIGARS, CIGARETTES AND CANDY. HOP GOLD ALWAYS ON TAP. DELIVERIES AT ANY TIME. PHONE 41.
SHAMROCK BEER PARLOR

WE ARE CARRYING THE LARGEST SUPPLY OF LIQUOR IN TOWN . . . . WE HAVE ON HAND THE ORIGINAL THREE STAR HENNESSEY BRANDY IMPORTED FROM FRANCE—ALL OTHER BRANDS OF POPULAR WHISKEYS, BRANDIES AND HIRAM WALKER GIN (WE FURNISH ICE FOR THAT LONG COOL DRINK)
SKAGWAY LIQUOR STORE

PILOT VERNE BOOKWALTER believes he may have discovered a hitherto unknown lake 20 miles west of here, as a result of a recent air voyage during which he sighted a sizeable lake not to be found on available charts . . . .

FROM AUGUST 4, 1934

HINDENBERG, GERMAN PRESIDENT, PASSES . . . death came quietly to a man who said that he had in his eighty-six years gone through every hell of war . . . . When word came, Chancellor Hitler and his cabinet were prepared, for in a guarded session last night, the cabinet adopted a decree revoking a law of 1932 under which the President of the Supreme Court would become President during the interim . . . .

PLEBISCITE ORDERED BY GERMAN GOVERNMENT . . . . It was expected that the plebiscite . . . . will have the double purpose of expressing the induction of Hitler as president and of passing on the politics of the Nazi government.

FAULKNER GIVES FAVORABLE OPINION ON SWIMMING POOL. A week ago a letter was sent to Mr. H.L. Faulkner, attorney for the city of Skagway [who lived in Juneau, the capital] asking him to investigate the legality of erecting a dam on the proposed site . . . . [S]ince the stream was frequented by a few trout, it might be illegal to dam it . . . . [T]he main points [of his reply] are as follows . . . . "I would hardly think that the little creek at Skagway would be considered a salmon stream and in my opinion there is nothing against erecting a dam for the purposes of making a swimming hole."

BRRR! THESE WATERS ARE COLD . . . . [W]e decided to . . . run some readings with a thermometer borrowed from Mr. Jack Taylor, the local weather man. Last week we hiked to Long Bay to find that the water, both in the fresh water stream leading into it, and the bay itself, was 50 degrees Fahrenheit . . . . [T]he warmest water around Skagway was registered at 56 degrees and 58 degrees in the Reservoir and 57 and 58 degrees in the Lake, with a low of 55 ½ in the stream from Upper Lake Dewey. Tuesday we went up to the Old Swimmin' Hole . . . and a temperature of 49 degrees was taken . . . Then over to the glacial Skagway River where 43 degrees established a temporary low. Temporary it was, for when we journeyed to the creek south of Sullivan's originating in a spring north of town, the icy depths of 41 ½ clutched at us . . . . We concluded our scientific survey with a trip to the wharf, and a temperature of 46 ½ degrees was the main reading [in the Bay] . . . .

Advertisements

"LAWYER MAN"
William Powell
Joan Blondell
Wed. Fri.
BROADWAY THEATRE

FOR SALE
ESSEX COACH
Good running condition,
New Rubber and Batteries
$100. 50% of
freight prepaid
Lt. Vida
Chilkoot Barracks

From August 8, 1934
PRESIDENT ROOSEVELT NATIONALIZES SILVER . . . .

ROOSEVELT SAYS NEW DEAL HERE TO STAY . . . .

Editorial Page
A REPUBLIC FAST BECOMES AN OLIGARCHY WHEN VOTERS REFUSE TO GO TO THE POLLS . . . . One month from today, the voters of Alaska must pass to the polls to give expression to their political thought. We, the editors of THE MIDNIGHT SUN, are members of no party but The People; we hold no brief for any system but Democracy; we put forth no candidate but The Best Qualified Man . . . .

Call the PC police! Hey, editors, what about The Best Qualified Person? O.K., this was almost 70 years ago.

From August 18, 1934
NEW COZY BEER PARLOR INSTALLED. With the addition of the new beer parlor in the rear of his cigar store, Louis Emmanuel begins to take on the aspect of a local tycoon. His new beer parlor has just been papered and painted throughout and equipped with indirect lighting . . . .

WARREN GRIFFITHS, the two editors and the printer's devil [Roger] returned from the Portage Thursday afternoon. There were no old blind fish apparently for they returned home with vast volumes of nothingness in their fish baskets.

About 40 miles north of Skagway the First and Second Portages were located on a series of small lakes and streams in British Columbia that formed the headwaters of the Yukon River. They'd acquired their names during the Gold Rush, when they were feasible spots for crossing the Yukon's headwaters in order to proceed north. We reached the First Portage (usually known simply as the Portage) by train. Although it was not a regular stop, the conductor and engineer, forewarned, would stop to drop us off with our food, fishing gear, and blankets, and would stop to pick us up on the way back from Whitehorse a few days later. A log cabin owned by Ken Hannan—the only one within miles—

was located some thirty or so feet from the tracks. Mr. Hannan generously lent his usually empty cabin to fishermen like us.

A hundred yards from the cabin a fast stream, barely wadeable, flowed into a small lake. Ordinarily the mouth of the stream contained some eager and unsophisticated greyling, which would take the flies offered by some eager and unsophisticated fishermen like us. Evidently this time they were all out to lunch somewhere else.

LOCAL LONGSHOREMEN STRIKE. The local longshoremen staged a strike last Wednesday when the Princess Louise was in port. The men demanded an increase in pay which the local agents had no authority to meet, without conferring with their superiors. The men struck in the morning at eight and again at six P.M., but both times they returned to work.

By this summer and thereafter, Lew and I must have been working as section hands, since we weren't involved in the strike.

ADVERTISEMENTS

LOST. One small kitten. An indistinguishable, brownish, black, Persian answering now and then to the name "Penny." See Marge or Evelyn Goding.

ANNOUNCING the opening of LOUIE'S NEW BEER PARLOR featuring Rhinelander Beer in the Wooden Keg, your assurance of a NEWER, BETTER glass of REAL beer. AT ONE P.M. TODAY a 15 gallon keg of RHINELANDER BEER goes on tap. FREE as long as it lasts.

—BEGINNING SATURDAY, Aug. 18, absolutely NO BEER will be served IN THE FRONT of the store. The FAMILY and MAIN ENTRANCE to the new beer parlor is ON THE SIDE. Come down and inspect this NEW, CLEAN PARLOR. THE BEER IS YOURS. Catering to Whites Only. LOUIE'S CIGAR STORE.

Catering to Whites Only. Looking back, it's easy to spot Big Trouble in Paradise, to perceive the vicious serpent in the Garden of Eden. What did the editors, particularly the righteous Backwoods Philosopher, think about this? Why didn't they reject the ad? I'll postpone to a later chapter any attempt to deal with questions like these. Meanwhile, let's keep in mind that on the periphery of my memories of Skagway a poisonous serpent lurks.

From September 1, 1934

Editorial Page

One more issue will mark the finish of this summer's edition of the Midnight Sun.... We wish to extend our warmest thanks to: MOTHER, who has typed each one of our stencils, who has done most of the real work, whose frequent censorings and corrections have saved us much embarrassment and without whose aid the paper would be a complete financial failure.

We went on to thank nine others, including Cathryn Hahn, Vic Sparks, and Master Roger Dahl, the Printer's Devil, as well as Our Steady Advertisers, Our Subscribers, All the Courteous People "whose names have been unintentionally left out of the paper," and "the Great Number of People who have done us numerous small favors..."

From September 5, 1934

SCHOOL YEAR OPENS WITH 68 STUDENTS. Late sleepers were awakened yesterday morning in Skagway by the familiar pealing of the Public School Bell....

Editorial Page

IT'S BEEN FUN, PUBLISHING THIS SO-CALLED PAPER OF OURS.... We've had loads of experience, but, unfortunately... it's rather difficult to hand the bill collectors a draft on your experience... So we're not particularly sad because it's time to call a halt....

10. Off Broadway

Our walk, which began with the WP&YR offices and its white-collar employees, ends at The Shops and its blue-collar employees. Although both groups—white collar, blue collar—might claim to be the heart of the railroad operation, I have no doubt that a shutdown at The Shops would close the railroad a lot sooner than a shutdown at the other end of Broadway.

Here are the machinists, master mechanics, boilermakers, plumbers, electricians, carpenters, painters (not necessarily different people) who keep the railroad's buildings in repair and its equipment functioning up to par. Here is home for the locomotives (steam, of course), passenger cars, freight cars, flat cars, gondolas, and other rolling equipment. Here the locomotive engineers, firemen, conductors, and brakemen assemble to begin their trips, and to here they return. Here the section hands assemble before heading off to maintain the first dozen miles or so of track.

How our visiting sociologist will make sense of all this I can't say. Engineers usually start out as firemen; conductors as brakemen. On the passenger trains, conductors and brakemen wear white shirts, ties, and blue suits. Engineers, brakemen, and all the rest wear overalls or coveralls, blue, tan, brown; blue shirts; no ties. Members of the two or three most skilled occupations are respected as excellent craftsmen. Whether any of these differences fortify social status more generally is harder to say.

❦

I leave these arcane matters to our sociologist in order to describe an incident involving two master mechanics at The Shops that should be recorded in the Guinness Book of Records for World Honors in the Practical Jokes Competition.

As I've already mentioned, George Rapuzzi worked at The Shops. His metal bench with vise, lathe, tools, and the like was twenty feet or so away from that of Jack Hoyt. Jack had arrived in Skagway from Seattle in 1929 and by the mid-Thirties had become a skilled boilermaker, his work essential to the maintenance of the steam locomotives, among other things. Jack and George became good friends, probably even teasing one another with rude jokes in the way American males often do.

One day at work when Jack touched his bench he received a shock. An electric shock. It lasted only a second or two. Some days later it happened again. And from time to time thereafter, at entirely unexpected moments.

Jack could find no explanation for these unpleasant episodes—no visible loose wires grazing his bench, indeed nothing at all that could account for the sudden jolts of electricity. Nor could his friend George, who instead teased Jack with inventing the whole thing.

Determined to uncover the source, Jack made an excuse one afternoon for staying on after the whistle had blown that marked the end of the day at The Shops and provided a general end-of-working day signal for the entire town. Jack spent most of the evening and on into the morning hours disassembling his bench, piece by piece. At last, cunningly concealed in the metal foot of his workbench and nicely soldered to make a neat fit, he found a wire. The wire disappeared under the wooden floorboards. Jack proceeded to pry them up, one by one.

The path they traced under the floorboards led directly to . . . his friend George Rapuzzi's workbench. There it ended at a craftily hidden button that George could press when no one was looking his way.

Jack left the button and wire in place, put back the floorboards, retouched them lightly with the usual dust, disconnected the wire at the foot of his bench, and put his bench back piece by piece.

One more necessary task had occurred to him, which he completed before leaving for his few remaining hours of sleep.

Like all the Rapuzzis, George was a hard and conscientious worker. But as Jack well knew, George regularly took a morning break around 10:30, when he retired to the outhouse for twenty minutes or so. There he smoked a cigarette or two, allowed his digestive tract to complete its designated function, maybe glanced at the Sears Roebuck calendar conveniently nearby in case of a paper shortage, and in due time emerged, rested, refreshed, ready for the hard work that awaited until lunch.

Jack's final task the night of his great discovery was to cut a hole in the back wall of the outhouse, just below the seat and just large enough to insert a grease gun. Several mornings after Jack had identified the source of his occasional electrical torments, George retired to the outhouse around 10:30 for his usual R & R. After a few minutes Jack followed him out with a loaded grease gun.

Shortly thereafter George uttered a bellow of pain, surprise, and anger and sprung out the door, his pants down, and desperately wiping his filthy bottom.

Jack later claimed that after finally recovering from *his* shock, George said no word about it, nor did he ever.

They remained friends.

Jack became mayor of Skagway during World War II, moved in 1959 to Whitehorse and ten years later to Hawaii, where, unable to give up on railroads, he worked on the building of another small railroad for sugar cane and tourists. George continued on as a machinist at the shops until 1965, and on retirement employed his talents in operating the Soapy Smith museum, collecting "antiques," ran a taxi business. And, maybe, gave up on practical jokes.

❦

As our sociologist continues to poke around, he runs across three more groups relevant to his inquiry: the dock workers, the section hands, and a group I'll call characters, eccentrics, and (other) marginals. The Indians to one side, these three groups probably occupy the lowest rung on whatever status-ladder may exist in Skagway.

I know something about the first two groups because Lew and I worked summers on the dock and later on the railroad section, and I knew nearly all the people in the third group. But in order to bring our sociological inquiry to a close, I'll save most of that for later.

Both types of work, our sociologist soon learns, are relatively unskilled: they require, as the saying goes, a strong back and a weak mind. (Though before we rush to conclusions, let me add that one of our fellow section hands, Dean Story—Alice's kid brother—is as smart as anyone I will run across in my later life, and a lot more likeable than many.) Both are mainly summer occupations. During the rest of the year the number of dockworkers and section hands is tiny. Few of the men who work on the dock and the sections are married: their low hourly wages and the limited number of working days provide an annual income insufficient to support a family. In fact, the docks are about the only place in Skagway where itinerants are occasionally employed, and even there itinerant labor is uncommon: the White Pass regards these jobs as places reserved for its own Skagway men and "local boys"—students in high school and college like Lew and me.

If you grew up in Skagway, you didn't aspire to end up as a section hand or dockworker—or, if you were a girl, to marry one. As starting jobs they were acceptable, but little more; and the few who remained in them, earning enough in the summer to squeak through the winter, were likely to be viewed as somehow lacking in the get-up-and-go spirit that gained the general approval of other Skagwayites.

The Rapuzzi House

Except for "Indian town" down by the dock, it doesn't matter much where you live. We learn that a rivalry had once existed between kids from the North end and the South end of town, but by the time we arrive it seems to have died out. And anyway, that rivalry, such as it was, had nothing to do with those sociological favorites, status and class. In our time, even the difference between North enders and South enders has become more legend than reality.

Our first house, the Tropea house on Seventh avenue, was, I suppose, in the North end, the second, the Rapuzzi house on Second Avenue, only about two hundred yards from the Bay, was definitely in the South end. I have no memory of the difference in location mattering one whit.

An Evening on the Front Porch

So what conclusions does our visiting sociologist draw from all of this? I'm inclined to retire him to his study to mull over his observations and interviews.

My own answer is provided by a photograph bearing the inscription "Past Exalted Rulers B.P.O. Elks 431 Skagway Alaska May 25, 1935."

In 1935 the Masons and the B. P. O. E. (a.k.a. the Benevolent and Protective Order of Elks), are the only active fraternal orders in Skagway. Both are mainly White Collar in their membership. The Eagles, which had been more of a Blue Collar club, seems to have fallen on hard times; its clubhouse looks to be one more of Skagway's abandoned buildings.

There are thirteen men in the photo of the Past Exalted Rulers of the Elks lodge in Skagway. All are wearing suits, with vest, shirt, and tie. All except two are wearing hats: three caps and the rest fedoras. In the front row, sitting, from left to right are:

Oscar Selmer, barber.
Will Blanchard, auditor's office.
George Miller, General Manager, W. P. & Y. R.
Howard Ashley, Manager (The Shops?).
V. I. Hahn, Superintendent, W. P. & Y. R.
Lee Gault, Sr., brakeman, ticket agent, telegrapher,
   W. P. & Y. R office.
Standing, in the back row, are:
W. J. Mulvihill, telegraph operator, train master, mayor.
Frank Suffecool, owner and operator of The White House,
   a residence for tourists.
Father G. Edgard Gallant, Catholic priest (sans chapeau).
Dr. Peter I. Dahl, physician (also).
David Stevenson, railroad conductor.
Arnold Gutfeld, auditor's office.

Well, make of it what you will. As in all human associations, social distinctions did of course exist in Skagway. As I've already mentioned and will return to later, as elsewhere in the Territory and the States an invisible barrier separated Indians from whites. And I hardly need to say that among the whites our visiting sociologist would surely have detected some modest social differences based, as elsewhere, on differences in education, occupation, income, performance, and judgments about character.

Nonetheless, taken all in all, Skagway was probably the most egalitarian place I've ever known.

11. The Midnight Sun, 1935

Revenues from *The Midnight Sun* proved too meager to pay tuition and living costs at the University of Washington for both Lew and me. So the next summer I became the sole editor and publisher. Putting out the paper was full time: I didn't try to combine it with working on the section.

I kept in shape by running every day, and on Sundays hiking up to Upper Lake Dewey, about 2500 feet above the town. I'm amazed to recall that by the end of the summer I was actually trotting up the steep trail. One Sunday, still full of energy when I reached Upper Lake, I continued to hike on up to the lower peak of Dewey mountain. When I discovered on my return that I was going to have to jump over a low cliff that on the way up I'd managed earlier to crawl over, for the first time in my life I came to grips with my mortality—and my foolhardiness. The second time was nine years later at an observation post in France. But that's another story.

From June 26, 1935
Editorial Page

Here, friends, is another summer and the third volume of THE MIDNIGHT SUN . . . . It is a small town newspaper; it is written for the people of this neck of the woods . . . It is your paper, to read, to criticize, to contribute toward, and perhaps to enjoy. We ask of you only one thing—tolerance . . . .

So here we go again.

PRODIGAL YOUTH, LOST IN FOG OF LEARNING, RETURNS HOME. The young bloods of Skagway, who left last fall to spend nine intensive months swarming knowledge into their blood cavities, have been swarming home the past several weeks, covered with book larnin', weariness, and sox in need of mending. Among them are: Harley

Baker, who returned from his third year at Mt. Angel Seminary in Oregon and dashed out again to a job on the Yukon River. Joe McCann, who likewise returned from Mt. Angel and now drapes over a pick handle on Section One. Dave Melbourn, ibid. (without the pick handle). Alice Smith, who just completed her first year in pre-law at the University of Washington and is now home studying Blackstone. Ed Gault, who is taking art but has not gone arty at the U. Rod Johnston, who has been toying with volts and amperes and whatnot in electrical engineering at the same school. Marge Goding, now a not-so-sedate-school-teacher-to-be, who finished her last year at Yankton College, So. Dak. Evelyn ditto, who swings a mean shorthand after a year at business college in Portland, Ore. Winnie Sipprelle, who returns to sunnier climes after her freshman year at Alaska College in Fairbanks. Lewis Dahl, who after four years of looking at parasites, white rats, test tubes, and ankles got his Bachelor of Science at the University of Washington this year.

Friends of Mr. Wilfred Goding are glad to hear that he is now attending summer school at Yankton College, So. Dak. Wilfred has recently been teaching in South Dakota.

From June 29, 1935
TOURIST SEASON OPENS IN SKAGWAY . . . .

A.F. OF L. HEAD GIVES F.D.R. NEW N.R.A. PROPOSAL . . . .

JOE LOUIS-LEVINSKY BOUT SCHEDULED FOR AUGUST . . . .

ITALIAN PEOPLE FAVOR WAR WITH AFRICAN ENEMY . . . .

From July 6, 1935
U.S. TO MAINTAIN NEUTRAL STATUS IN AFRICAN CONTROVERSY. Washington, July 5 . . . . [T]he State Department has decided to reject all pleas for American interference in the Italo-Ethiopian crisis . . . .

AFTER THE GOLD RUSH   83

LEGION HEAD COMPAIGNS AGAINST "RED DANGER." National Commander Belgrana of the American Legion today warned that agents of Communism are seeking through propaganda and sabotage to wreck the foundations of American government in hope of fomenting a revolution . . . .

The editorial page narrates "The Story of the Blue Salmon and the Red Salmon." This thinly veiled parable informs us that the Blue Salmon, who were the rulers, remained so stuck in their ancient practices that when they encountered a fishing net blocking the entrance to their traditional spawning stream, they persisted in their old ways. But a little Red Salmon led a revolt and insisted on trying a new stream. So the Blue Salmon perished and the Red Salmon survived. In due time the red Salmon "developed into a Great Race of Salmon . . . so good that their history books said their blood was blue." A thousand years later the history repeats itself. ["The first time as tragedy, the second time as farce."] And lo! ". . . all perished but a breed of Ignorant Salmon—called the red Salmon—who revolted and went up the newer stream."

O.K., Skagway: Wake up!
O.K., Bob, shut up!

FROM JULY 13, 1935

The lead story is:

DOG, LOST IN MOUNTAINS, RETURNS. It is not news when a town finds a dog. But when a dog finds a town . . . . Last week, King, aged, loved, and respected member of the Dahl family, made news by finding Skagway and home after a five day search.

King set out at his master's heels Sunday morning to climb the peak of AB mountain. But the eleven year old dog tired quickly, and soon he dropped far behind. He kept on going up to the peak, but on his arrival there he was not content. He must find his master. So he struggled on.

When he did not show up that night, his master retraced his former day's journey but he could not find the lost dog. The dog, faithful in his desire to find his master, kept on. He did not return Tuesday. People all over town expressed their regrets. He was believed dead.

He wandered on all day Wednesday. He reached Inspiration Point Mountain. As the train rumbled by, several men looked up and saw the tired old fellow looking at the train from across the river. When they got home, they reported seeing him, and next day two men set out to find him.

In the brush beside the track, as the train carrying the searchers rumbled by, lay the dog, tired, hungry, weak, but nearing home. His searchers looked; the dog walked. On and on. Suddenly a great black Engine came bearing down on him. He saw human beings; he whined, and they picked him up and they carried him to his master.

Gaunt and tired, he wagged his tail, and whined. He tried to bark. He rested, and then he walked with them to Skagway. He saw . . . his home, and he whimpered as he walked through the door.

After King rested for a week and ate the best meal we'd ever given him, he recovered fully. If anything he was a even a bit more vigorous than before. Several summers later, however, he died, lying on the front porch where he had passed many happy hours with his family. Lew and I carried him over to the Skagway River and buried him in the sandy soil of the riverbank.

From July 17, 1935

Editorial Page

Skagway needs three things immediately and badly: she needs a tennis court, she needs a swimming pool, she needs a playground.

Shows how much influence our earlier editorials had on the town.

BENNETT PICNIC BIG SUCCESS. The annual Presbyterian Sunday School picnic held yesterday at Lake Bennett was voted a huge success by every one of the 240 people present. Leaving here at 8:15 yesterday morning . . . the train ran into cloudy weather immediately. Beyond the summit, however, sunshine was the order of the day; enough breeze blew to keep the mosquitoes in harness. After lunch, the children's races were held. These were followed by a ball game . . . . Horseshoes occupied the time of the older men, as did also brave attempts to plunge into the cold waters of the lake . . . .

From July 20, 1935
BERLIN TO PERSONIFY NAZI IDEOLOGY . . . .

NEED FOR CONSTITUTIONAL CHANGE—SEC'Y WALLACE . . . .

LABOR PARTY ORGANIZATION OUTLINED. Moscow, July 19. A plan to build a worker's party in the United States was outlined by William Foster once Communist party candidate for president . . . .

JAPANESE NAVY TO COMMENCE WAR GAMES . . . .

THOUSANDS PERISH IN CHINESE FLOOD . . . .

SKAGWAY GIRL TO MAKE WORLD TRIP . . . . Miss Christine Johnston, daughter of Mr. and Mrs. H. L. Johnston, will take up duties in the beauty parlor of the Empress of Britain September 19 and will leave subsequently on a world cruise . . . .

When we were both around thirteen, Christine, was my first girlfriend. She died in Anchorage in 1978 at the age of 63.

From July 27, 1935
FRANCE, ENGLAND MEDIATE IN AFRICAN CRISIS . . . .

GANDHI TO SEEK INDIAN SUPPORT OF ETHIOPIA . . . .

PRESBYTERIAN BIBLE SCHOOL STARTS MONDAY. The annual Presbyterian Bible School will commence Monday, Rev. F. Klerekoper announced recently.

Our much loved and admired Griff was no longer in Skagway. Alas!

From August 3, 1935
FRANCO-BRITISH SOLUTION, ETHIOPIA, REJECTED . . . .

SWEDEN TO LET ETHIOPIA ARM . . . .

ITALY ORDERS MORE MOBILIZATION . . . .

GERMANY AGAIN STRIKES AT PERSONAL LIBERTIES.

Advertisement
GENUINE NESTLE
PERMANENT WAVES
Beauty Work and
  Haircuts
Edith Hukill Phone 68

From August 10, 1935
WAR CLOUDS RUMBLE AS SETTLEMENT OF AFRICAN AFFAIR VANISHES . . . .

ENEMIES OUT TO GET LONG—HUEY LONG . . . .

PEACE GROUP ASKS FOR SANCTIONS AGAINST ITALY, PACT VIOLATOR

PERSONALS. Pat Farwell and Joe Goding, fishermen, are expected to return from the Portage this afternoon, with a good catch, after two days fishing.

MISS LOTTIE GAFFY, who has been teaching for the past year in Nome, arrived in Whitehorse Thursday and will return here soon.

From August 14, 1935

BIG SLUICE BOX ROBBERY, ATLIN. What is said to be the first sluice-box robbery to occur in Atlin in 25 years took place last Saturday night . . . .

From August 17, 1935

NATION MOURNS LOSS. WORLD STUNNED BY DEATHS. UNIVERSAL SORROW AT DEATH OF ROGERS AND POST, KILLED IN AIRPLANE TRAGEDY AT POINT BARROW.

Point Barrow, Alaska, Aug. 13. Will Rogers and Wiley Post were killed last night when their plane crashed near an Eskimo village 15 miles south of here . . . .

ROOSEVELT'S TAX BILL PASSES . . . .

IL DUCE AGAIN TURNS DOWN PLAN FOR PACIFIC SETTLEMENT OF DISPUTE . . . .

ITALO-BRITISH RIFT PREDICTED . . . .

MRS. HANNAN THRILLED AT WIMBLEDON. "Yesterday I had another one of my wishes fulfilled," wrote Mrs. K. B. Hannan recently [to Mother, no doubt]. "I went to Wimbledon and saw tennis as it should be played . . . ."

MISS GAFFY HOME AFTER YEAR IN NOME

From August 24, 1935

BRITAIN, FORESEEING STRUGGLE, POLISHES UP WAR MACHINE . . . .

NOTICE! "Superintendents and School Boards of Incorporate City Schools: I have a letter from . . . the Territorial Commissioner of Health to the effect that, since smallpox is very prevalent in Southeastern Alaska, is will be necessary for all pupils and teachers who have not been vaccinated within three years to be vaccinated before schools open this fall . . . . Commissioner of Education." The above letter is self-explanatory . . . . I will be in my office every morning and afternoon, so that all can be vaccinated before school opens September 3. Dr. P. I. Dahl.

Editorial Page

THE EDITOR'S AFTERNOON OFF . . . . Intent on giving ourselves and our readers a rest, we decided to quote something really good from somewhere . . . .

And about time, too! The editorials in the preceding four issues were titled, respectively, NATIONALISM, INTERNATIONALISM, WAR, PACIFISM. Well, those were the big issues of the day, weren't they?

From August 31, 1935

MIDNIGHT SUN IS THIRTY-SIX YEARS OLD. Most Skagwayites believe that *The Midnight Sun* made its first appearance a half dozen years ago when three youthful editors tried a fling at journalism. Surprisingly enough, *The Midnight Sun* first made its debut in 1899 . . . . The Klondike Nugget was a newspaper first published in the latter part of May, 1989, in Dawson, the early issues of which appeared in the form of typewritten bulletins displayed on a board in the street. It was only a month after The Nugget appeared, however, that a lively competitor made its bow. This competitor was entitled "The Midnight Sun." They both fought fiercely for subscriptions and advertising, until the demise of our namesake, when the field was left clear for The Nugget.

From September 7, 1935

ITALIAN WALKS OUT AS CONCILIATION GROUP IS NAMED . . . .

WAR WILL REMAIN IN AFRICA, SAY FRENCH OFFICIALS . . . .

ITALY MAY ASK BRITAIN TO GET OUT OF EGYPT . . . .

YOUTH MIGRATION SOUTH BEGINS. The clarion call of Education is causing another annual outflux of eager youths bound for the vast and sanctimonious halls of learning. The University of Washington makes the strongest bid, with seven Skagwayites . . . Miss Winnie Sipprelle . . . will leave for her first year at Washington, . . . [after] her freshman year . . . at

Alaska College in Fairbanks . . . . Miss Alice Smith will be bound for her sophomore year at the University . . . . Mr. Rodney Johnston . . . will get his degree from the U. in electrical engineering this year . . . . Mr. Ed. Gault will also be leaving . . . for his third year at the University; he is also an art major . . . . Mr. Lewis Dahl . . . will be bound for the University of Pennsylvania Medical School in Philadelphia.

Editorial Page

"The time has come," the Walrus said, "To talk of many things . . . ." And so the third volume of the Midnight Sun comes to an inauspicious close . . . . Our editorials must have irritated many people, but no one verbally indicated the fact. We are ready to admit that our lack of analysis was astounding; that many editorials were puerile and inadequate; that often they completely missed the point. The only thing of which we are reasonably confident is that the subjects that we tried to analyze, even if incompetently, are currently of tremendous importance . . . .

We hope, too, that the Midnight Sun has somewhat helped to weld the community together . . . .

To those people who insist that we should print news of social affairs, we offer a stern reprimand: . . . the editor of any Skagway paper that attempted to cover accurately all social affairs would be given an unqualified blue-ticket within a month. He couldn't possibly keep from injuring tender feelings . . . .

The summer has been a great experience, and more fun than any other summer we can recall. The swiftness with which it has passed is evidence of our real enjoyment.

We have learned much about human beings, in the particular, and in the general. We have probably lost a few friends, and perhaps gained a few.

We are looking forward to another summer and more discussions.

" . . . of shoes—and ships—and sealing wax
Of cabbages—and kings—
And why the sea is boiling hot—
And whether pigs have wings."

12. At School

Quite possibly the first Skagway resident to make a lasting impression on me was Lottie Gaffy, whom I encountered a few days after our arrival when I took my assigned place in the sixth grade. She was a tallish woman in her late thirties, with a strong jaw and straight hair, not exactly pretty. She was unmarried then and remained so throughout her life.

In school she was stern and no-nonsense, and one of the best teachers I ever had. She hadn't changed by the time our next door neighbor Tom Tunley arrived in her class 15 years or so later.

The School

"Lottie Gaffy," he recalled some years ago, "was one of the great teachers! No doubt about it! She had discipline in her room and one was obliged to work. I spent time at my desk facing one of the back corners in the room for talking when I should have been listening. I now have no complaints." [20]

I soon had a lesson myself. I'd envied the ability of some of my new acquaintances, boys in particular, to make an ear-splitting whistle by blowing vigorously through the ends of two fingers. One day that first spring in Skagway, as I walked back to school after lunch I tried to master the technique—and failed. I may have dawdled along the way and was a minute or so late to the schoolyard. A few seconds before I entered the school building I finally succeeded. Dizzy with success, and anxious to consolidate my gain, I thought I should try once more, just to be sure. I succeeded brilliantly with an ear-piercing blast—right at the door of our classroom. I entered the room on the heels of my screeching triumph. Every eye in the room turned on the culprit as he tried to slink to his desk. Including Lottie Gaffy's.

"Robert," said Miss Gaffy, "if you wish to act like a First Grader you can go down to their room and sit with them." She promptly led me there and explained the reason to a somewhat bemused first and second grade teacher.

The children around me hardly knew what to make of a huge boy squeezing into one of their small seats. Nor did I. Even more embarrassment was in store. Not long after I'd arrived among the first and second graders, the fire alarm sounded. A drill! I dutifully marched out, towering over my temporary classmates. I'll never forget standing outside with them, waiting for the order to re-enter. Nor will I forget Miss Gaffy coming up to me and saying, "Robert, you may now rejoin your class."

Though at first I strongly suspected that Miss Gaffy had turned on the alarm, in later years I concluded that she wouldn't have done so. She was strict, yes. Stern, yes. But never harsh or mean. On the contrary, as I came to realize in later years, behind her stern exterior was a warm and kind person who was dedicated to teaching and devoted to her students. Years later while I was in college and graduate school, I made sure we met during the summers when I was home. We were friends. I like to believe that she took

---

[20] From the Carl Nord documents.

some pride in my academic achievements, and I hope she knew that she had played a small but important part in helping to shape the person I became.

✺

Skagway Public School ran from first grade through high school, with twelve grades and about a hundred students, all in the same two-story wooden building. Through the eighth grade, one teacher presided over two grades in one room. The four grades of high school occupied the top floor, where students assembled in a single largish room that also served as a classroom for some subjects, though we walked over to one of the three other rooms for our classes in civics, algebra, Spanish, English, and whatever.

The average class size, as you can quickly figure out, was about nine—a little more in the early grades, a little less later on. The sixth grade that I joined in mid-January in 1926 had nine or ten students, who by my senior year had narrowed down to just six of us. I was in the Sixth grade in a room with the Fifth Graders, all under the firm control of Miss Gaffey. Lew was in the Seventh along with the Eighth Graders, both taught by Mr. Riordan, who also coached basketball.

By today's standards, I suppose, the formal education we received was pretty poor. My Spanish teacher was a man in his late thirties from Montana who for some bizarre reason may have been presumed to know Spanish because he was part Indian. As best we could guess, he studied the textbook at night in order to stay barely ahead of his students. After two years of Spanish, all that was offered, my grasp of the language remained dismal.

I made up for some of the school's deficiencies in other ways. Because I had expressed a strong interest in the law as a profession, Dad concluded that I had better know Latin. In later years I realized that if American lawyers were subject to a test of their proficiency in Latin that went beyond the standard phrases of legalese, almost all of them, including the eminent justices of the United States Supreme Court, would fail dismally. At the time, however, Dad's view seemed persuasive.

But Skagway High School, which barely squeaked by on Spanish, offered no course in Latin. Dad was aware that at least one Skagway resident—and, as it happened, a friend—surely would. This was the Catholic priest, Father Gallant, whom I've already mentioned.

Father Gallant readily—indeed, I think enthusiastically—agreed. So about one afternoon a week during the school year, I'd walk over to the Manse and spend two hours studying Latin. I can't say that I ever gained much capacity to read Latin, and I don't remember that we ever read any of the Latin classics. But combined with the trip over the Chilkoot Pass that I mentioned earlier, his mentorship in Latin left me with a life long admiration, respect, and affection for the man.

He was, I believe, a truly dedicated priest, yet one with not a trace of zealotry. I've often wondered whether he may have hoped for my conversion. But not once in all the time I knew him did he say anything that I could interpret, then or on later reflection, as an effort to persuade me to become a Catholic. As I mentioned earlier, I had already fallen away from the Presbyterian Church—thanks in part to the bigotry of Reverend Petersen—and was moving toward the agnostic humanism that I would later think through more carefully. By not seeking my conversion did he fail his obligation as a priest? I think not. I really don't know how what his parishioners thought of him, nor any personal or theological deficiencies he may have had, but for me he remained an example of a person deeply committed to making *this* world a better place.

In view of the scandals that have erupted over the sexual abuses committed by priests, perhaps I should add that in my presence he never once, by word or gesture, made the slightest advance that could be interpreted—then or now—as sexual in nature. Had he ever done so, I'm fairly certain that I would have detected it and reported it to Dad. Thanks to the crude sex-laden humor and comments by my companions in school, at play, in the locker room after hockey or basketball, at work on the docks or section, I was by no means ignorant of the possibilities. Nor can I recall any speculations about Father Gallant's sex life, whatever that may have been. Though I've sometimes wondered how such a robust and vigorous man dealt with his sexual drives, my reflections have left me without a clue.

In pursuit of his goal of improving the world around him, in 1931 Father Gallant created the Piux X Mission School, where Alaskan native boys and girls from around the Territory were housed, fed, supervised, and taught. Naturally he was the school superintendent and along with several nuns he governed and taught the children under his care. To create and maintain the school took money, and on trips to New York and elsewhere Father G. employed his considerable charm, urbanity, and intelligence to encourage wealthy Catholics to part with some of their funds for the benefit of the school.

Occasionally on one of these trips he would visit Mary and me, and he remained much as I remembered him. He died in 1975 back where he was born, on Prince Edward Island.

❦

Despite his efforts and mine, I never did acquire a real facility for reading Latin. What I read under Father's supervision was more likely to be a passage from the New Testament than Caesar's Gallic Wars or Cicero's Orations. Thanks to him, my pronunciation was the Italianate Latin of the Church, with its soft "c" before "e" or "c"—*"dulce"* would be "dulche" not "dulke"—which no doubt made me sound off-base on the rare occasion when I might use a Latin phrase among friends and colleagues but proved to be a slight advantage when, many years later, I began to learn to speak Italian. I also acquired something of a grasp of—or at least an enduring interest in—the Latin origins of many English words.

My greatest triumph, which Father Gallant would have appreciated, came a half-century or so later when I was asked to serve as a referee at the Yale-Harvard football game. Well, a Yale-Harvard game. A contest had been scheduled on the morning preceding THE game, this one between the Yale Department of Political Science and the Harvard Government Department. It was to be touch football, and the players were to be drawn from department members, with maybe a few graduate students sneaked in. Although my knowledge of the rules was limited, to say the least, I was invited to serve as a referee, along with the head of the Harvard Department, Harvey Mansfield, Jr. I was also asked—by whom I've long since forgotten—to award the cup to the winning team. The cup itself was a battered coffee mug that one of the secretaries sacrificed for the honor of the occasion, which I covered in aluminum foil.

Harvey Mansfield and I each did our best—that is, to help out our own teams—and it happened that Yale won.

On the way driving over that morning, as I reflected on what might be appropriate for the occasion, I was suddenly inspired by this thought: what could be more fitting than a brief oration in Latin? However, about all I could still remember from my studies with Father Gallant were some of the mottos in Latin that headed each chapter of the textbook. "Sic semper tyrannis . . . Dulce et decorum est pro patria mori . . ."

Holding the cup high over my head I gave my presentation speech in Latin—a dozen or so mottos strung together, impressive if you didn't know Latin, utterly senseless if you did. Where at an earlier time a gathering of Yale and Harvard faculty members and graduate students would doubtless have included many who would have known enough Latin to catch on, by this time in the evolution of American education none, it seemed, did. "Wow!" I heard one of our graduate students say, "I didn't know that Dahl could speak Latin!"

Alas, my fraud was soon exposed. At a post-game party—post THE game, of course—a graduate student approached me with the inevitable question: "Professor Dahl, how did you learn to speak Latin so proficiently?" I noticed a smile crossing the face of a friend who was standing near us. I knew that she happened to be proficient in many languages, including, certainly, Latin. I confessed the truth—without, I may add, feeling any remorse for my trick.

Thanks to Father Gallant some of the other deficiencies in my formal education at the Skagway Public School were also remedied, at least in small part. A priest who served with him at the Pius X Mission helped me to learn some of the elementary principles of chemistry. One summer another provided three or four of us with a bit of tutoring in French.

In addition to Father Gallant, Skagway offered one other invaluable means for my formal education: the little public library. Like several other families in Skagway and many others I've known since, ours was a family of *readers*. We all read voraciously: Mother, Dad, Lew, Roger, and I. And although the Skagway Public Library was small, its books were a treasure trove. In addition to its own acquisitions—frequently in response to readers like Mother—some of its books were supplied through a program of the Carnegie Endowment in aid of small town libraries like that in Skagway.

Indiscriminate as my reading surely was, by the time I'd finished high school I had probably read as widely as most of my fellow students at the University of Washington.

In fact, during my years in college and graduate school, I never felt that the Skagway school had left me with any significant comparative disadvantages. Some years later I did come to regret my lack of training in foreign languages and in mathematics, gaps I then tried to fill with courses and self-instruction.

The biggest academic challenge for me at the University of Washington was to speak up in classes that were much larger than any I had ever experienced. To find myself in discussion courses with twenty, thirty, forty, even fifty others was pretty intimidating for someone accustomed to six or seven. It was probably my junior year before I gained the confidence I needed. Fortunately for me, my exams and written work more than compensated for my silence in the classroom, and the boy from Skagway ended up his senior year (here comes a confession prompted more by vanity, I fear, than any need to the record the fact here) with a straight A record—well, except for one B in a sociology course, of all things!

❊

I've been using the term *formal* education to describe my schooling in Skagway. That was probably not much different from what I would have received at the time in many another very small town in the United States.

The most distinctive parts of my education were my activities outside of school. What I learned there was probably more important than what I learned, or didn't learn, at school.

13. At Work: on the Dock

The summer when I was twelve I started working as a longshoreman.

❦

Is this the opening sentence of a Dickensian novel? *In the tenth year of his life, Oliver began work in a Lancashire cotton mill, beside his widowed mother.* Or maybe my attempt to emulate a Mary Lee Settle story about West Virginia? *When he was twelve, like his father before him, Llewellyn descended into the depths of the coal mine where he was to spend his working days for many harsh and dreary years to come.*

Well, not exactly. Every boy and girl in Skagway worked summers at one job or another. They might have weeded gardens; or worked in their parents' store, like the Kirmse boys and the Richter sons and daughter; or as they moved into their 'teens, labored on the docks or the railroad section. For boys, a summer job usually meant manual labor. For girls, as I recall, there were fewer paying jobs and so more of them helped out around home.

But full time idleness, a summer vacation without working, was out of the question.

During my previous summer when I was eleven, I'd worked seven or eight hours a day, as I was needed, weeding, hoeing, digging, and what not at Skagway's only commercial garden. It was located up north of town, so I'd ride up and back on my bike—two round trips, since I came home for lunch. The garden—we called it Clark's farm—was owned and worked, except for an occasional summer helper like me, by Henry Clark, the owner. Henry Clark was one of the old-timers, having arrived in Skagway in '97 from Wisconsin; and as far as I now remember, he was a good and decent man. So I don't hold him responsible for the lasting effect that working in his garden was to have on me: over that summer I developed a detestation for weeding gardens that never diminished—as Mary and Ann were later to discover when they invited me to participate in weeding our gardens. Though I did some weeding in later years, I pretty much hated it and with the passage of time I managed to weasel out of the hateful task at every opportunity; almost any excuse would do.

❈

So the next summer I turned to longshoring. Although twelve was a bit early to start such hard manual labor, I was tall for my age, wiry, and strong. And in those days, of course, child labor laws didn't prevent me.

Fortunately, the opportunity to find work coincided perfectly with the school's summer vacation. The boats that brought the tourists (we usually called them "boats," not "ships," though they were 300 feet or so in length) also carried freight stored several decks down below in the hold. Like Skagway and the White Pass railroad, the towns in the Yukon—Whitehorse, Dawson, Mayo, and others—were almost completely dependent for their basic supplies, from food to machinery, on shipments from "Outside." The only way to transport these supplies was by boat. Because of tariffs and customs duties, freight that was to remain in Skagway would come by boat from Seattle via the Alaskan Line; if it was headed across the border into Yukon Territory, it normally came from Vancouver or Prince Rupert via the Canadian Pacific and Canadian National lines.

Freight for the Yukon, which sometimes included an impressive number of cases of good Scotch whisky, would be shipped by rail to Whitehorse, where some of it might be loaded onto riverboats and transported down the Yukon River to Dawson, Mayo, and other towns along that vast river. Although the headwaters of the Yukon originated in a series of small streams and lakes a little more than twenty miles north of Skagway, where the continental divide also served as the national boundary, at Whitehorse it turned into a wide river that was navigable during the ice-free summer months. (We found it intriguing that at the Summit, the continental divide, some of the streams flowed south, became the Skagway River, and reached the Pacific 20 miles away at Skagway. A few steps farther north, they began their northward and westerly flow and finally joined the Pacific—the Bering Sea—2,000 miles later.)

Though a trickle of freight came into Skagway from September through May, when a boat would arrive about once every two weeks, most of it reached Skagway when the tourist boats were arriving two or three times a week during the summer. Although only one or two longshoremen might be needed for nine months of the year, in June, July, and August the need surged. As a result, during the summer essentially unskilled laboring jobs were available, which meant that males without full time employment could find work. These consisted of a few locals like Herman Garmatz, who lived alone in a cabin up on Dewey mountain, a few drifters from Outside, whose numbers increased in the summer of 1930 with the beginning of the Great Depression, and Skagway boys otherwise unemployed. Because the management of the White Pass tried to take care of "their own"—Skagway was, after all, a one-company town—Lew, Rod Johnston, Wil Goding, I, and other local boys had an edge.

Determined to avoid the tedium of weeding gardens, the summer when I as twelve I decided to see if I could get work on the docks.

❦

In Skagway a longshoreman[21] worked for one of two employers: either the White Pass or one of the shipping lines—the Canadian Pacific, the Canadian National, the Alaska Line. If you were moving freight from the ship's hold to the White Pass warehouse on the dock—let's just call it unloading—you were hired by the boat, that is, the shipping line. If you stacked freight in the warehouse or, later, loaded it from the warehouse to a freight car—let's call it storing and loading—you worked for the White Pass.

To get a job unloading from the boat, you would ordinarily arrive at the dock early in the morning of the boat's arrival, usually six or seven a.m. It might increase your chance if you got there in time to help tie up the boat by pulling in a casting line and securing the attached hawser to a cleat on the dock, after which you would stand around until the Third Mate showed up. You and the other potential hirees would gather in a semicircle—the Shape-Up—around the Third Mate, who would point to the

---

[21] Although the terms longshoreman and stevedore are both used for persons who load and unload ships at dock, we invariably spoke of longshoremen and longshoring.

lucky ones and say, "O.K., you're on." If he chose you, the Third Mate would write down your name, and you would then retrieve a hand truck from the warehouse—a two wheeled affair, metal wheels, no rubber tires in those days—about four feet high and capable of holding 300 pounds or more. You'll see their lighter, rubber-tired descendants today around warehouses or large retail stores.

Unloading might take place in one of two ways. In the usual mode, ship's sailors would load freight into a sling, which would be hoisted by winch and dropped to the dock, gently if the winchman was skilled, roughly if he wasn't. There, a longshoreman would move the freight on to your hand-truck. Your challenge was to get just the right balance for that particular load, whether it was three crates of eggs, four cases of canned goods, or five bags of flour. Though it was much safer to allow your arms to take the full weight, as you quickly learned that position also made the task much more tiring. Yet if you tried to reduce the weight on your arms by holding the truck more nearly upright, you could easily spill the contents, as most beginners did sooner or later when they hit a rough spot on the dock's aged planking.

You would push your loaded truck to the appropriate place in the warehouse, where longshoremen working for the White Pass would unload and stack its freight. Then you'd head back for another round-trip, and so on, and on, and on. You'd have an hour's break for mealtime, when I would usually mount my bike and head home for a huge but hasty refueling before returning to the dock for the rest of the day.

❂

I said that unloading might take place in one of two ways. The alternative was "The Slip."

This contraption, which had been designed by V.I. Hahn, the Superintendent of the White Pass, was an ingenious device for taking freight from ship to shore. To grasp what it was like, you might imagine a bridge about five feet wide and forty or fifty feet long that forms part of a dock. The inner, landside end of the bridge is securely hinged to the dock. The outer edge of the Slip, which almost touches the hull of the ship to be unloaded, can be dropped down by a winch. The action is something like a drawbridge in reverse. Now imagine a ship with a large door located on the hull at the level of the hold where the freight is stored. The Slip is lowered to the level of that door, extended, and firmly secured. Voila! We have a bridge running directly from the dock to the hold. Easy passage for a hand truck!

But there's still more to the ingenuity of the contraption. Because the ship's door into the hold is lower than the level of the dock, the Slip is angled downward. How far downward depends on the tide. Pushing an empty truck down the slip to the hold is easy, almost fun. In fact, at lower tides you'll have to hold it back.

But it would be something else again if you had to push your truck back up from the ship's hold to the other end of The Slip at dock level. With a heavy load—say four or five cases of canned goods—at low tide it could become practically impossible.

So here's the ingenuity of the thing, and the reason, I guess, for its name. Running down one side of The Slip is a big chain with large teeth spaced a foot apart. The chain is hitched to a motor that rotates it from the hold up to the far end at the dock, where it disappears to reappear down at the bottom end, the ship's end, of The Slip. After you've loaded up your handtruck in the hold, you push it to the door and on to The Slip, where one of the large teeth catches the axel of your truck. And up goes truck, with you holding it up from behind. A superb saver of human energy!

At high tide and a small angle of elevation, The Slip is great. When the tooth grabs the axel of the truck and the handles are suddenly thrust down, you get quite a jar. But you learn to handle that. And the easy walk up the slip, holding the handles at a nicely balanced angle, is almost a pleasant challenge.

But as the tide gets lower and the angle steeper, The Slip becomes a form of legalized torture. (No child labor laws, remember). It grabs your truck like an angry monster and thrusts down the handles as if it wants to tear them out of your hands and pull your arms off in the process. You begin to approach the monster with fear and loathing.

Now if the tides were those of Rhode Island, where my tide chart for July shows a maximum of 3.8 feet at full moon, The Slip would almost be sheer pleasure. But Skagway is located at the end of a hundred mile inlet from the pacific, and the tides are fantastic—regularly 15 feet and at full moon 20 feet or more. If V.I. Hahn ever tried out his creation, which I doubt, I'm certain he never did so at low tide.

Fortunately, most boats were unloaded the conventional way, but even so, torture by means of The Slip occurred all too often.

❦

If a Third Mate came to know you and concluded you were a reliable worker he might give you a preference in hiring. But getting a job unloading was not only chancy, it was necessarily of short duration. The tourist boats usually left the night they arrived, or maybe the next day, so unloading had to be completed in a day. And that was it until the next boat arrived two or three days later.

The better job, then, was working for the White Pass, loading freight from the warehouse to the boxcars. For one thing, loading was steadier work, because once the freight was in the warehouse, moving it into the boxcars could be spread out over several eight-hour days. It was easier—no torture by The Slip. And once the Wharf Master decided you were "a good worker," he would try to hire you regularly. You could begin to count on work as long as there was work to be had.

The Wharf Master was Wirt Aden. He had been born in Rotterdam in 1866 and christened Weert Dirk Aden, and so he must have been around 60 when I began working on the dock. Wirt Aden was a short, rotund man, unmarried, who lived with a couple that, according to the cruel gossip reaching my not so tender ears, formed with Wirt a *ménage a trois*. He was not, I think well liked, particularly by those who worked for him, to whom he seemed short-tempered and arbitrary. But if you wanted steady work, you had to stay on his good side, mainly by giving proper deference to his superior station—the respect, as I now realize, that as a short, fat, friendless man he probably felt he lacked.

❦

If you worked for the ship, unloading, you were paid 85 cents an hour, with no extra pay for overtime, the same rate whether you worked six hours or twelve. If you worked for the White Pass, stacking the freight in the warehouse or, later, transferring it to the boxcars alongside the warehouse, you earned 65 cents an hour, which increased after eight hours to time-and-a-half at 98 cents an hour. Overtime, as I've said, was infrequent.

By today's standards the wages look pitifully small, though less meager if converted into today's dollars. But when one out of four workers became unemployed in the Lower Forty-Eight during the Depression, we were fortunate to have any work at all.

The first summer Wirt Aden sometimes hired Lew, but I mainly worked for the ship, unloading. Even so, often I wasn't chosen by the Third Mate during the Shape Up. I must have looked too young. So my earnings were skimpy.

But the next summer and thereafter, Wirt Aden hired both Lew and me pretty regularly.

※

As we became bigger, stronger, and more experienced, we sometimes managed to get ourselves hired for two of the most backbreaking jobs I've ever had. At one of these we worked for the White Pass unloading bags of silver-lead ore from the freight cars, the open Gondolas, as we called them. For the alternative job we would be hired by the Third Mate of the coal freighter to work down in the hold shoveling coal onto slings that were then hoisted up and dumped into the coal car on the dock.

The silver-lead ore came from a mine at Mayo up the Yukon River. There it was put in 110-pound bags, which were then moved on to paddle-wheel steamers that made their way up-river to Whitehorse, where it was transferred to the Gondolas. With two men working on opposite sides of the sling, you could choose to work either singly or as a pair. It was much easier and less tiring, of course, to lift the 110 pound bags if you worked as a pair; but the two of you each working alone could load the sling faster and so might gain more time to rest between loads. In either case the work was exhausting.

At least it wasn't much dirtier than our usual tasks on the dock. Unloading coal, on the other hand, was just as backbreaking as unloading the ore sacks, but it was fouler work: after a few hours we looked like minstrel show performers ineptly smeared in black-face. Except for meal-breaks, you worked steadily until the ship was fully unloaded, which sometimes might take sixteen hours or so, after which you made your weary way home to bathe and sleep for ten or twelve hours.

Though we hated unloading coal, we never turned down an opportunity to take on that disagreeable task.

※

Work on the docks came to an end for Lew and me around 1936. The reason was a bit ironic.

As a strong supporter of unions I had thought for several years that a union of the dock workers in Skagway would be desirable, though I should add that my efforts came to nothing more than the loose and unfocussed talk of a young radical. Harry Bridges, on the other hand, did more than talk. Like many of his union officials and organizers, this colorful and dynamic Australian-born head of the International Longshoremen's Workers Union was widely and probably correctly believed to be a Communist. Whatever the truth of that belief, employing the harsh clout of a several long, tough strikes Harry Bridges had successfully organized the main port cities of the West Coast. Alaska was not to be ignored. To the consternation and probably the astonishment of the officials of the White Pass, in due time ILWU organizers not only showed up in Skagway but found there a receptive audience among the dock workers, and after some turbulence and strike activity secured the recognition of the Union by the White Pass.

One of the first actions of the new Skagway local of the ILWU—quite appropriately, I had to admit—was to convert the longshoremen from casual laborers to a core-group of permanent employees.

The casual laborers who would no longer be employed during the summer on the docks included, of course, Lew and me.

Our longshoring careers had ended.

14. At Work: the Railroad Section

So Lew and I returned in June with no prospects for working on the docks. Luckily, and no doubt thanks to the paternalism of the White Pass, we did find work on the railroad section, at 50 cents an hour, eight hours a day, five days a week.

The railroad's 110 miles were divided into about ten sections, each with its own gang of six, eight, maybe ten men. Our section began at the ends of the two stretches of track terminating in Skagway. One stretch

White Pass Railroad train 17 Miles from Skagway

passed through the center of town on Broadway, the other diverged north of town, hugged the mountain on the eastern edge of the town, and went to the very end of the town dock where we had previously worked as longshoremen. Our section ended a dozen miles or so up the valley to the north.

To reach the part of the track where we were to work that day, the six or so members of the section gang would meet by seven a.m. at the north end of town, up near The Shops. To reach the day's working area would ordinarily be too far to walk, so we'd mount a hand-car—nowadays you see them mostly in old photographs or cartoons—which would be propelled by two men pumping up and down on the handle-bars. For longer distances we enjoyed the privilege of riding on a "Casey" (properly, a Casey Jones), which had a gasoline engine.

Our straw boss, who worked alongside us, was Dean Story. Dean had been a classmate of mine in the sixth and seventh grades, as best I can now remember, who soon thereafter dropped out of school for reasons I never fully understood, because he was as smart as anyone I've known and came from a family that was by no means indifferent to the importance of education.

Although section work—"gandy-dancing" we sometimes called it[22]— was dull and often fairly hard work, it was also highly sociable, at least if you had the right crew, which Dean generally did. Our main tasks were removing and replacing damaged rails or, more often, damaged ties. Our main tools were a hand-shovel and a sledgehammer. We used the shovel for "tamping ties," a task at which two men stood opposite one another on each side of a railroad tie and pushed their gravel-laden shovels under the tie in order to level up the two rails. As you can imagine, the work was mind numbing, to which one antidote was gabbing. We gabbed a lot.

---

[22] I had long wondered whether the expression in some distorted way referred to Mahatma Gandhi. But I now learn that a "gandy dancer" is. "1. A railroad section-hand or track laborer; one who lays railroad tracks, grades roadbeds, or digs drainage ditches. *Since c1915 hobo, railroad, and lumberjack use. From the rhythmic dancelike movements made by laborers straightening rails and smoothing gravel. In the South the work was often accompanied by group chanting, the rhythm assuring that the laborers would simultaneously apply their crowbars to straighten the track.*" Harold Wentworth and Stuart Berg Flexner, *Dictionary of American Slang* (New York: Thomas Y. Crowell Co.: 1975).

Heading up the Tracks

Putting down a new rail was something else again. The ties and rails would be brought up on a Gondola and put to one side. After leveling up the surface with gravel, we'd lay down the ties, set the rail across them, and spike it down. Like tamping ties, spiking was a two-man operation, in which two men would face one another from opposite sides of the tie and the new rail, each swinging his hammer in sequence with the other man in order to drive down the spike on his own side of the rail. Spiking required skill, lest you come down too close to the rail and damage it—not exactly something you wanted to do on a new rail—or too far away and miss the spike. But after you learned how to swing that hammer, the rhythmic action was rather satisfying, maybe something like two fast-moving dancers moving in unison. Gandy-dancing. After eight hours of spiking, even with occasional intervals to set the ties and rails—or just gab—and a break for lunch, you'd end up weary but pleased with your day's work.

One summer Lew and I grew to be very good at spiking rails.

Just north of Skagway the rail line crossed over the Skagway River on a trestle bridge and then a few miles later crossed back on another bridge. When construction began back in 1898, I imagine that the granite mountain hugging the river on the east posed an excessively difficult barrier for those few miles, while the stretch on the west side of the river was easier. So: a brief loop across, up a bit, and back across to the east side. But the Superintendent V. I. Hahn and his son, Vic Jr., a trained engineer, now decided that this brief detour was unnecessary and the track should run straight up the east side right next to the mountain.

The mountain, however, was full of curves—as full of curves, someone said, as Mae West. No matter. With his surveying instruments and a helper, Vic, Jr. laid out the line.

In addition to the voluble and often amusing Dean Story, our straw boss, the fellow workers I remember best were:

Paul Wilson, a Tlingit Indian, married, father of two girls who were several years my junior. Paul had been educated in a mission school down the Coast. He was intelligent, thoughtful, and companionable. If he had been white, Paul could reasonably have hoped to occupy a white-collar job in the White Pass headquarters. He might even have gone Outside to a university and become a lawyer, doctor, dentist, engineer, or whatever. But Skagway's racially based caste system had put careers like these beyond his aspirations and possibilities. In a later chapter I'll come back to Paul and the caste system in which he was ensnared.

Joe. Counting the Tlingits, perhaps close to a hundred people of color, as we would say today, lived in Skagway. But only two of these were African-Americans, or, as we said then, Negroes (and I have no doubt some said Niggers). One was Mrs. Couture, who had been born in Dawson and moved to Skagway, where she lived a quiet and no doubt lonely life, occasionally working at house-cleaning and similar tasks. The other—as far as I knew they rarely if ever spent any time together—was Joe, who lived by himself in a cabin up at the north-end and worked on the section.

At the time I knew him Joe must have been in his sixties, still strong and vigorous. He was calm, self-confident, ready to talk, easy of manner. His account of his early life, which I believed then to be true, as I do now, was along these lines: The son of ex-slaves, in his 'teens or early twenties he had, like many others, headed out to the Southwest—present day Arizona or New Mexico, as I recall. There he became a U.S. Marshall, an experience that may well have contributed to the quiet self-confidence that marked his manner and that one-day he exhibited to us in the following fashion.

Working with us that summer was one *Punchy Anderson*, who had served in the Army at Chilkoot Barracks fourteen miles down Lynn Canal and when his hitch ended had come to Skagway looking for work. Whether he or others had given him the nickname "Punchy" I never knew, but, so at least he claimed, the name came about during an earlier hitch in Hawaii where he had been a lightweight boxer, indeed, so he said, a winner of the title match for the entire Island. In the course of his boxing career, his story went, he had become a little punch-drunk, more or less permanently. Or at least so he claimed. But Punchy was, we had all concluded, a bull-shitter and we were never sure how much of what he said was truth, how much was bullshit, and how much was a mixture of the two.

For reasons I don't remember, one day at work Punch took umbrage at something Joe had said. The essence of their exchange went something like this.

Punchy: Joe, you'd better not show up down at my end of town tonight, or anytime else, for that matter. I just might have to pull out my pistol and let you know you're not wanted there.

Joe: Punchy, I hadn't planned on going down town tonight. But if you'd like to come up to my house, I'd be glad to let you in. I've got a butcher knife, and Punchy, you show up in my house and I'll cut you wide, long, and deep.

That ended the conversation. Needless to say Punchy never accepted the challenge.

The rest of us were so infuriated by the way he had behaved toward Joe that the next day, out of Punchy's hearing, Dean concocted a conspiracy that we would all agreed to play along with. The next day:

Dean: (To Punchy and others). Do you guys know I've just bought myself a new '38 pistol? I'm good, too. I could hit a bulls-eye at fifty feet. No trouble. I bet I could even shoot off the heel of someone's shoe without hitting the foot. Hey, Punchy, I'd like to try. Maybe tomorrow? You stand about thirty feet away, and I'll show you that I can shoot the rubber heel off your boot without leaving a trace on you or the rest of your boot. I'll even have a new heel put on! How about it, Punchy?

Punchy: Naw, Dean, that's not a good idea. You might miss. Let's just forget it . . . O.K., Dean?

And so it went, with Dean still insisting at quitting time that he'd like to try it the next day.

Dean's plan was to bring his pistol, loaded with blanks.

The next day, Punchy didn't show up for work. Nor the day after. Or the next.

When he finally did return to work, he was quieter than he had been. He left town not long after.

In June, 1937, I returned from my first year of graduate work at Yale and, like Lew, who was back from his second year in medical school, I went to work on the railroad section.

During that first year at Yale I had taken a seminar on Modern Political Theory where we had read a great deal of Marx. By the end of the year I was already moving toward the view I later formulated in my dissertation, one that recognized his originality but found his theory seriously flawed in all its major components, from the labor theory of value to his theory of the state.

One morning during that summer of 1937, Dean and I were engaged in the supremely dull task of tamping ties, gandy-dancing. During the later part of the morning I chose to overcome the boring nature of

Lunch in the Sun

our joint task by setting forth some of the rudiments of Marx to Dean. I explained how, according to Marx's theory, the "surplus value" he was creating by his work that morning would go to the shareholders of the White Pass Railroad. Obviously, like all members of the working class he was being exploited by the railroad.

No doubt Dean was all the more easily convinced about this exploitation because it fitted into some partly formed view along these lines. But not satisfied, the budding (and arrogant?) intellectual/academic/big-talker felt a need to do more. After all, in that seminar and others didn't we also try to search for the flaws in the views we so assiduously studied? So during the remainder of the morning I led Dean through the errors in the theory of surplus value. This exercise no doubt left him not only perplexed but, as I came to realize later, rather insulted. Talk about exploitation! A guy with his fancy education had exploited his friend and co-worker—made a fool of him, in fact, by first convincing him of one thing and then turning right around to convince him of the opposite.

It was now noon. We walked back toward our lunch-buckets, which we'd put down beside the track a few yards away. As we walked, we encountered Lew, who was also heading toward his lunch-bucket.

"Lew," Dean firmly announced, "your brother Bob is an inter-lectual horse's ass!"

He was surely right. As the years rolled on, I often thought about that morning. I came to hope that, more than he could ever have known, Dean Story had helped me to change from what I surely was at the age of twenty-one.

15. At Play

If I was sometimes bored, as I must have been, I no longer remember it. Having excess time on my hands to mope about is not among my memories. Instead, what stands out most clearly to me now is how very active we were, not just in school and at work but also during the ample time we had left over for our own amusement, entertainment, sports, recreation, play, call it what you will.

True, from June to September, most days we were busy at work. And from September to June we were in school five days a week.

Yet work and school allowed plenty of time for other activities. School began at nine and let out at three. In the Dahl household, the evenings, Sunday through Thursday, were strictly for homework: no television in those days, and because of the mountains, radio reception was so bad Dad concluded that it was pointless to own one.

Aside from our standard chores like splitting wood for the stove, mowing the lawn, shoveling the snow off the walk, and whatnot, during our free afternoon and weekend hours we usually engaged in sports. In the early fall we sometimes played a bit of touch football—we had no uniforms, helmets, or pads, so touch was about all we were equipped for—and we turned to baseball in the spring. But our main winter sports were basketball and ice hockey. We began basketball in October down at the White Pass Athletic Club, a big, old, drafty, wooden building with a shower-room, a basketball court, and even some bleachers. Our biggest challenge was to find enough players to man— if that word fits—two teams. Sometimes the high school basketball team would have to draw on eighth graders to fill out a second team. For a real contest, one that might even attract a few onlookers to the bleachers— the balcony—we would play against a men's team that had quickly been patched together without a lot of practice.

The Basketball Team
Back: **Myself, Bud Blanchard, Walt Siprelle, Ed Richter, Jack Lee**
Front: **Mr. Thoemig, Lew, Rod Johnson**

In December we began ice hockey. A wooden frame made of two-by-twelves fitted to the dimensions of a hockey rink would be set up on the town's baseball field and when freezing weather set in the area would be flooded by damming the creek that ran nearby. With Nature's help we had a rink.

I possessed enough energy, strength, size, determination, stamina, and competitive drive to serve me well enough in all the sports and physical activities I would engage in throughout my life—fishing, hiking, crew, handball, squash, tennis, canoeing, swimming, sailing, hunting, kayaking (which I took up only a few summers ago)—but I lacked the coordination required for a really top-notch athlete. As a result, I was never a star, even in the Skagway bush leagues. In both hockey and basketball, Lew, who was better coordinated than I, would play forward while I had to content myself with a defense position, never scoring many goals but sometimes stopping one from the opposing team.

For both of us, hockey was a new challenge. Although Lew and I had learned to roller-skate back in Iowa, on our arrival in Skagway neither of us knew how to ice-skate. The fall after our arrival we each ordered a pair of hockey skates from Sears, Roebuck or Montgomery Ward (a.k.a., Monkey Ward), and after the rink froze over we both began to learn how to skate.

The town somehow managed to scrape three boys' teams together, named the Sourdoughs, the Alaskans, and the Vikings. (Why the Vikings, I can't say, but at the time I never thought to question the name). Despite my obvious ineptitude on the ice at the beginning of that first season, the shortage of available boys insured me a spot on one of the three teams, the Vikings, I think. Seeing that I could barely stand up on the ice, let alone skate down the rink without tumbling over, I was made a goalie. The goalie, I should add, was provided with no special protection, no shin pads, no breast pad, no facemask, no helmet.

In the only action I can now recall from that first season, I see a forward from the opposing team swiftly bearing down on me. As he pushes the puck deftly from side to side with his hockey stick, he eludes our Viking defense and sweeps the puck up and off the ice straight toward the goal—and, what is more scary, straight toward the goalie. I pray that God will take mercy on me and employ His awesome power to deflect the puck away from me—and as an extra favor, dear God, would You also keep the puck out of the net? I should know, of course, that God is busy at more important things, and that if God happens to be in a stern mood my highly self-centered request might even earn me some well-deserved punishment.

Whatever: lacking the divine intervention I have so fervently requested, the puck hits me squarely on the upper lip. I shout in pain. The game stops. I rush over to the side of the rink, take off my skates, put on my hiking boots, and, shouting in pain as I run, I dash all the way up to the hospital. Luckily, Dad is in his office. He calms me down, takes a quick look, and reassured by what he sees, puts in a few stitches and sends me home.

Although in later years I came to understand that my asking God to intervene in such a trivial matter would surely be viewed as an impiety, my fervent but failed prayer may have helped to begin the erosion of my faith and nudge me toward a more skeptical stand. Some years later, after my first three days of combat in the fall of 1944, I developed an outlook that I later came to describe as a kind of prudent and hopeful fatalism.

Happily my teammates welcomed me back despite my dramatic demonstration of incompetence as a hockey-player. Of course, without me they would have been short a player. Anyway, my hockey skills soon reached about the level of the others.

❀

Sports weren't our only recreation. During the winter months someone might invite friends, both boys and girls, to a party at the host's home. These parties were pretty tame, judged by later standards. At some, we danced to the tune of a waltz or fox trot played on a crank-wound Victrola. Necessity forced me to learn to dance—though to my regret I never did reveal much promise as a ballroom performer. Sometimes we played the exciting game of Post-Office. When by the luck of the draw I found myself briefly assigned to the darkness of a clothes closet together with a randomly selected female partner, I gained my first opportunities to kiss a girl. What fun, especially with the right girl! Boys and girls also began dating, even "falling in love"— which for me consisted of fairly brief periods of the sort that adults dismiss as puppy love.

Compared with dating after the sexual revolution of the Sixties, our relations were pretty innocent. When you were about to say good night as you left the girl at her door, you might engage in some passionate necking—that was what we called it—under the stars. During the summer months, those ardent midnight kisses might take place under a sky that even at midnight was almost as bright as day, thus exposing the behavior of the ardent couple to anyone who might still be up and around.

Yet even though being seen necking in public was embarrassing in those days long ago, and anonymity is impossible in a small town, that didn't seem to stop, or much inhibit, our midnight necking. But that was as far as we went— as far as I went, anyway. When I left high school, I was still a virgin. I'm pretty sure Lew was too. Although I can't be certain about other boys, I'd guess that my friends were also; at any rate, in all the loose talk and bragging boys engage in, I never heard one of them claim that he'd lost his virginity.

At a different (higher?) level of local culture, town dances would be held from time to time at one of the few suitable sites, like the Elks' club.

Almost everyone came, young, old, and in-between. Kids like me would sometimes gaze with surprise at a pair of gracefully dancing old-timers who might have reached the advanced age of fifty. And surprise! surprise! they could actually be the parents of one of my friends.

In mid-winter, a "Days of '98" evening would sometimes be staged at the White Pass Athletic Club. It would run something like this:

When we pay our entry fee at the door of the White Pass Club we receive a packet of fake money. Gaming tables, we can see, are set up on the basketball court: blackjack, poker, even a roulette table that has somehow been preserved from the real days of '98. With casinos a commonplace now, none of this may seem exotic, but in the Skagway of my boyhood a public gambling hall is little more than a faded memory from an earlier era.

The dealers are in costume, and so are many of the guests. As midnight approaches the peak moment arrives with a performance of "The Shooting of Dan McGrew." In case a benighted reader may not recognize the classic known in those days throughout Southeastern Alaska and the Yukon Territory, this work is a poetic drama composed by a onetime Whitehorse resident, Robert Service, who in the time and place I'm describing is deemed the rightful Poet Laureate of Alaska, the Yukon, Canada, and, in a not uncommon view, the entire English-speaking world.

As best I can remember at the Days of '98 evenings I always end up losing all the fake money I had started out with. Could that be why I never became attracted to gambling for money? Hmm.

Some years later the Days of '98 would be converted to a hokey summer entertainment for the tourists. But at the time of which I write they were just a hometown diversion for Skagwayites during their long winters.

So our days and nights, with their long hours of daylight in the summer and their long hours of darkness in the winter, were packed with activity.

Sometimes a curious tourist would inquire, "How do you manage to get through the long winters?" In response to this perfectly reasonable question, I found it hard to keep from smiling. How could I possibly explain Skagway life to Outsiders? The town was not without its problems but, to the best of my present memory, boredom was not among them.

16. A Journey to Goatland

"Play" may not be the most appropriate word for what was probably the most strenuous, exhausting, absorbing, and memorable of our activities: our trips up into the mountains hunting Rocky Mountain goats—and, by accident rather than design, a wolverine and a grizzly.

But before I turn to these episodes I want to acknowledge that some readers may be offended by the blithe manner in which I describe the killing of wild animals, particularly, perhaps, the beautiful and inoffensive Rocky Mountain goats living far up on their peaks totally innocent of any harm to human beings. For reasons like these, after leaving Skagway I began to feel that I no longer wanted to hunt. I'll say something more about this change after you've had a chance to read my account of one of our goat hunting expeditions.

That said, I don't want my later views to influence my accounts here of hunting trips I made many years ago. To do so would be to falsify my recollections of the way I experienced those events.

The hunting season for Rocky Mountain Goats opened on August 20 and closed, as I recall, at the end of October.

Dreaming of Glory,
Age 10 or 11

So as the opening day neared, Lew and I would begin to plan a hunting trip, maybe adding a few more days to a week-end or squeezing in the trip during the first week of September before school started or, a few years later, before we headed out to college.

Not long ago I discovered a narrative that I wrote for my English Composition class at the University of Washington near the beginning of my Junior Year. I'll present it here. Although the old-timer is an obvious concoction, the goat hunt I describe here is an accurate account, in the main, of the trip Lew and I had made that fall, just before heading off for the University of Washington. In the original version, my partner, who was, of course, Lew, is referred to as "you." After reflecting about changing the "you" to "Lew" I decided to keep it just as I wrote it at the age of 18. "You," dear reader, will be the you as you might imagine yourself at about the same age.

I said it was an accurate account, in the main. One minor change from the real story: "You" will shoot the wolverine, whereas in fact I was the killer. Perhaps I assigned it to "you" because my pride in having shot a wolverine—an event of extreme rarity even among the most experienced hunters—was mixed with shame about the wanton destruction of this rarely seen animal. I also constructed an ending that brought our trip to a swifter and more fitting conclusion than the grueling climb down that mountain that we actually made. But here it is as I wrote at the age of 18.

Dahl, Robert A.
Comp. 54
Oct. 9, 1934

A JOURNEY TO GOAT-LAND

The word "goat" has almost no tinge of the romantic in its intension. It connotes a dirty, smelly, unintelligent beast that gives, on occasion, abominable milk, a frequent frightened bleat, and an exhibition of supreme stubbornness.

An invitation, therefore, to hunt goats would be received with a great indifference, if not hostility, by the ordinary city inhabitant or rural farmer.

Why, then, should a few scattered persons jump excitedly about and rave enthusiastically upon such a suggestion?

The secret lies in the fact that to this small group the term goat is mentally modified by the description, "Rocky-Mountain." Have you ever seen a Rocky-Mountain goat in its natural environment? The probability that you have is not great; smaller yet is the chance that you have hunted them; and even less possible is it that you have shot one.

Let us, then, go on a Rocky-Mountain goat hunting expedition in Alaska; more specifically, near Skagway, in Southeastern Alaska.

For, there, hunting goats is not only always a difficult task; it is often also somewhat of an art and a science. There, goats are not plentiful—not because of man's ruthless slaying, but because of a greater ruthlessness, that of Nature. The mountains near Skagway appear green and peaceful in the summer, and white and peaceful in the winter, but while goats can live on green pasturage, they cannot exist on ice and snow. And so they are not easily discovered, and hence not easily shot. That is why goat hunting frequently is an art.

Before we leave on this, your first goat-hunting trip, let us ask an old-timer what characteristics constitute this elusive animal.

First, he will say, the goat has an uncanny and remarkable agility, and an unparalleled ability to keep his footing on treacherous ledges and rock-slides that would lead his lesser enemy, man, to inevitable death. His home in the summer months is in the peaks where, with vision of telescopic keenness, he watches every movement in every valley for miles below. His keenness of sight is, indeed, a precious heritage and a protection equaled only by his agility and speed.

"Truly wonderful how these goats can see," the old-timer says. "I remember once seeing a goat above me on a peak, a peak so high that only with the aid of my field-glasses could I really be sure that what I saw was a goat. I would walk slowly away from the peak, my back to the goat. Suddenly swerving about, I would train my glasses on him and watch him come to a halt. The farther away I walked, the more he moved, always a bit upward, but always keeping me in sight. Each time I turned around he would stop moving. With his naked eye he could discern my actions and tell my face from my back, while I could scarcely see him without the glasses."

The endurance of the goat, too, is great, as the old-timer will tell you with a smile, which proves that he has been foolish enough to attempt testing his strength against that of an animal which only a hawk could successfully race to the peaks.

An interesting characteristic of the goats, we learn, is their antipathy for and fear of the Bighorn sheep, which always drive them from the ranges.

Instead of living amicably together on the same slopes, as we expect, they are never found on the same feeding grounds.

Interesting, too, are their habits of movement, a knowledge of which, we learn from the old-timer, is a *sine qua non* in goat hunting.

"The most important thing," he tells us with a gravity which reveals its importance, "is that they come down at night and go up in the morning—and morning begins at midnight. I remember once seeing a herd of five goats amble slowly down a peak, to bed down for the night in a wide basin holding a lake. Already it was darkening; the goats were a full half-mile away; we were dog-tired. So, instead of obeying the cardinal rule of goat hunting—'Never wait: hunt your goats when you see them!'—we waited until morning, that is, until three o'clock, to go after them. By four we had arrived at the spot where they should have been. We looked cautiously over a ledge. Below us the valley was dotted with white figures which we vaguely made out in the dim light—it dawns early in Alaska during the summer—as white rocks, nothing else. No goats were to be seen and we cursed ourselves roundly for having let them slip through our fingers."

But that, we assure the old-timer, should suffice as a description, for we are anxious to get to the mountains, and listening to his tales only increases our avidity.

And so with twenty-pound packs on our backs—we must travel light, as you painfully learn when we start the real hiking—we hike that evening to a little cabin at the base of a vast mountain. Through a space between the logs which a careless builder left unchinked, we watch, as we lie rolled up in our blankets that night, the stars as they shine through a clear sky and, listening to the roar of the nearby falls, we drop softly to sleep.

At four we awaken and rush to the door. A pang of disappointment strikes us; where last night bright stars seemed to twinkle happily, now cold, gray clouds hover ominously around the peaks; a chill wind blows down the valley; in the peaks above it is snowing.

Undiscouraged, we start the long, tiring climb. Up, up, up we go; through pines, then alders, then underbrush we go. Finally we are in "the open." Eventually we reach a little valley high in the mountains, nestling among innumerable rugged peaks, all of which are potential homes of our prey.

A cold, biting wind tears at our faces and turns our noses a dull red. Carried with it and intensifying the bitterness of the weather is a half-sleet, half-hail.

We build a camp, so that we shall have something to which we may come that evening. We cut some wood. We pile all our food, save a few pieces of chocolate, on our blankets. And then, shouldering our empty packs, we start out on the search.

Soon our camp is a little gray dot far below us, and then, as we go over a pass, it disappears.

On we go, occasionally munching our chocolate, until finally we discover that there is none left to munch.

We travel on.

"This wind and all that snow on the peaks should drive the goats down," I mutter hopefully.

Mid-afternoon comes and goes. We begin to feel pangs of hunger. Soon we must turn back.

Suddenly I stop.

"I just saw a big marmot! Lord! It was big!" I exclaim. "See? There it is. But that isn't a marmot."

"What is it?" you inquire excitedly.

"Don't know. Maybe a coyote. No, it isn't a coyote."

I throw my rifle to my shoulder. The unsuspecting animal fifty yards away gnaws peacefully at a bone.

Bang! The little animal jumps, whirls about, eyes us excitedly.

I hear the click of your bolt. Bang!

Then a sound, an alarming, frightening, sickening growl, a half cry, half snarl that for a moment chills and terrifies us.

You have broken its backbone, thereby paralyzing its hindquarters; as it inches its way slowly along, it snarls at us menacingly.

We rush down to the spot where it lies growling wickedly. Although scarcely bigger than a small Airedale, the animal, which, I discover, is a wolverine, is vicious, frighteningly so. We wonder what would happen could he leap at us.

The wolverine turns its head slightly to one side. You shoot. It jumps feebly and lies still. It is dead. First blood!

But now, since you have killed the animal, you also must skin it; and so, dragging the wolverine behind a rock to shelter you from the wind, you unsheathe your hunting knife and slowly cut off the skin.

The job completed, you are about to put the pelt in your pack when I, who have been looking below, jump back and whisper excitedly:

"Goat down there—in the valley below us. Hurry. Quiet now. Hurry!"

You stuff the hide into your pack, which you shoulder, and seizing our rifles we run hurriedly down the hill.

Lower and lower we go, always keeping behind some ledge to keep the goat from seeing us.

Closer and closer.

We drop our packs and fall flat.

Inching ourselves along on our bellies, we crawl to the edge of a ledge, and there below us is—not one but three goats.

"I'll take the billy," you whisper.

"O.K. I'll take the nanny."

Click. Bang!

Up jump the goats excitedly.

Bang! Bang! Bang!

The hills echo with shot after shot, but still not a goat is wounded. Up they go. Up, up, up, to disappear over a "hog's back."

We look at each other disgustedly.

"Damn," I say disconsolately.

"You said it," you agree glumly.

Suddenly you straighten up and point. There in the distance are five goats.

Once again excitement reigns.

We work back to our packs, shoulder them, and hike cautiously on.

"How many shells have you left?" I whisper anxiously.

"Six. How about you?"

"Five. That's eleven. Have to get close. Can't miss *this* time."

Closer we come. Now we cannot see the goats. We climb up a slight ridge, and suddenly like a plummet you drop to the ground.

I do likewise, for there, only twenty-five yards away is a goat. Slowly we crawl along on our stomachs. We hear the anxious bleat of a kid. Closer, closer. I look up. I see two goats—no, three! four! five!

My heart pounds.

"Close enough?" you ask.

"Shoot!" I whisper.

You load. Click.

The goats suspect nothing and munch peacefully on.

A pause.

Bang! Your goat falls!

Then from every rock a goat appears! Not five goats, nor six, nor seven, but a dozen of them mill excitedly around.

I shoot and miss. Five more times I shoot and miss.

You give me your five remaining shells. The goats still run wildly around, not knowing in which direction safety lies.

Bang! Bang! Three left. Bang! Two. Bang! Still no success.

A long, careful, steady aim.

Bang!

Fur flies, the goat jumps—and runs lightly over a ridge. Missed! And no shots left.

We walk slowly toward your goat, which lies in a little green hollow, bleeding slowly. It is dead, shot through the neck.

"Sorry, old man," you say.

"That's all right. Congrats to you."

I look behind me, to see if any goats are still hovering about. There, behind a ridge, lies the goat at which I last shot—dead.

I run joyfully over to my goat and the hills echo with our cries of joy.

Two goats—our trip is a success!

With excitement still making our fingers tremble, we settle down to the not disagreeable task of skinning our two goats, and occasionally we place our hands on the warm flesh, somewhat to allay the chill which numbs our fingers. An hour's work sees the goats skinned and quartered, our packs filled and bulging, our hands wet and numb.

So, shouldering the incredibly heavy packs, we trudge slowly along in the rapidly darkening evening and, despite our backbreaking load, our feet are light and our thoughts are gay.

For we have been successful. We are goat hunters.

And after we crawl beneath our warm blankets that night, we lie by our fire hoping that Nature, which has a way of caring for all things, will treat gently the little kids that bleated so mournfully as their mothers lay bleeding.

Then with a weary sigh we turn over and fall asleep.

AFTER THE GOLD RUSH 125

Lew with a Goat

Myself with a Goat

A Full Pack

Reading this account all these many years later, I'm sharply aware of the changes in the world, and in myself. Some of you who may read these recollections three quarters of a century after the time I describe might well be revolted by the thought that we hunted such a beautiful and harmless animal for the sheer sport of it. And, dear reader, you're not likely to appeased by a meretricious appeal to utilitarian standards: yes, we did always butcher the slaughtered animal; yes, we did pack out every pound of meat, often more than a hundred pounds of it; yes, we hung it for a month or so on a meat hook in the walk-in freezer at the meat market, in the hope that it might thereby grow more tender; and yes, though we gave some of the tough and stringy meat to any friends who would take it, finally Mother cooked it and we dutifully ate it. So, yes: none of it was wasted. But no, I'll not employ that all too transparent disguise. I won't try to conceal an undeniable fact: our goat hunts were enormously gratifying experiences. Sorry.

And after returning from Europe in 1945 I no longer even wanted to put a rifle to my shoulder. To be sure, my not hunting had become an easy option, since the opportunities were immeasurably fewer than those presented in Skagway. But if the urge had remained, as it certainly has with fishing, I would probably have found ways to continue.

I should make plain, however, that my vanishing desire to hunt doesn't reflect an objection to it in principle. If others wish to hunt, obeying regulations and practices designed to preserve the species and its habitat, I don't contest their choice. It just isn't for me.

It wasn't until a reunion of Ann's family at Camp Allegheny in 1989 that I changed my mind about shouldering a rifle when we both decided we'd like to see if we could still hit a target, which Ann had learned to do at Camp Allegheny as a girl. Our enduring skills with a .22 made both of us proud. At the top of the bulletin board in my study where I now write is my "Official Fifty Foot Rifle Target" from that day. The five small black targets are nicely spotted with holes. I haven't picked up a gun since then.

I might mention one small change in my 1934 account that I might feel compelled to make today. In the sentence near the end I write that "our thoughts are gay" and shortly thereafter "we crawl beneath our warm blankets." How innocent I was at eighteen! Today a thirteen-year old might interpret my "gay" as a sly signal of a hidden secondary message. No, dear reader, when I wrote "then with a weary sigh we turn over and fall asleep," I meant just that!

However, as it happened, on that particular trip we did not "turn over and fall asleep." We were miles from our base camp, our food supplies, and our blankets. Darkness had set in, and we dared not try to make our way back. We were exhausted. One of the goats we thought we'd only scared away by a shot that missed was, in fact, lying on the other side of a rise, dead. So we had three goats, not just two. We left them where they lay, hoping that no coyotes would dare to approach the unguarded carcasses during the night. A few feet away from the goats we found a piece of mountain where we could sit, *even lie down. We built a fire. But, hungry as we were, we decided not to try roasting a cut of meat from our freshly killed goats, partly because any butchering we did would leave more blood and exposed flesh to attract predators. So we went hungry. The rocky ground on which we lay was hard and unforgiving. The night grew ever colder. The threatening clouds we'd seen earlier now dropped their stuff. At that altitude their stuff wasn't rain; it was snow. When we woke at dawn we were surrounded by a layer of white—not a lot but any at all was too much. We walked our stiff and weary bodies over to the ground where the goats lay. We sliced off their hides with our hunting knives and cut up each of the three into quarters, twelve quarters in all. We strapped the meat on to our backpacks. I also slung the wolverine hide over my shoulder. We staggered back toward our camp. Exhaustion soon overtook us. We began to stop every few hundred yards to sit, even lie down. In desperation, to my lasting regret and shame I threw the wolverine pelt off into the brush.*

An hour or so later we reached our base camp, built a fire, made coffee, stuffed ourselves from our food supply, repacked, and headed down the steep mountain. Darkness was approaching when from a low but steep twenty-foot cliff we finally sighted the cabin, our destination for the night. How could we get down to it? The branches of a spruce tree a few feet out from the cliff offered a possibility. We dropped our packs over the cliff, reached out, jumped, landed safely on the tree. We made our way down the tree, picked up our packs, staggered to the cabin, built a fire, pulled our blankets around us, and slept on the hard floor for ten hours or more.

After breakfast we crossed the bridge to the railroad tracks, headed down the fourteen miles to Skagway. And then, oh bliss! A train chugged up behind us. We waved. The engineer knew the Dahl boys by sight as we did him. He stopped the train. We got on and rode back to Skagway.

I can't remember the next day but I'd bet that after another long night's sleep we spent a good bit of it bragging to our friends about our wonderful goat-hunting trip.

When we headed off for college not long after, we must have left behind a lot of tough goat meat for our parents to dispose of. I never asked them what they did with it.

17. The Grizzly

It was on Roger's very first hunting trip that we shot our one and only grizzly bear.

Up to this point I've said a lot about Lew and me but very little about Roger. As I mentioned earlier, when we arrived in Skagway in January, 1926, Roger was barely past his third birthday. Seven years younger than I, eight years younger than Lew, Roger was the baby of the family.

Lew, however, was almost exactly a year older than I. (In view of the fact that we were all born in December about a week apart, I have concluded that March must have been a time of fertility not only for Nature but also for my parents.) Almost as soon as I could walk and talk, Lew became more than my brother; he also became my closest friend. Although we were different in many ways, our similarities and differences meshed well together. As boys we sometimes quarreled and occasionally we fought. But as we grew older the fights stopped entirely and our quarrelling became rare.

For a year or two after our arrival in Skagway, Lew moved in a circle of boys—Wil Goding, Rod Johnston, and others—who were older than I by a year or two; my pals were, like Mark Lee, closer to my own age and my grade in school. But about the time Lew reached thirteen and I twelve, once again we each became the other's closest friend, and his close friends became mine. And so we remained.

Roger, then, was our baby brother, our kid brother. Though we often played with him, the friends with whom he spent most of his free time were, naturally, kids of his own age.

One day during our first summer in Skagway, he and some of his young friends were playfully chucking rocks at several bottles out in the street when a fragment of glass flew up and struck him in the eye. Although Dad did whatever emergency surgery he could perform, he was not an eye surgeon. On his urgent insistence, Mother took him out to Seattle on the next boat and placed him under the care of an eye surgeon. The eye had been effectively destroyed, however, and after several years of annual check-ups in Seattle that revealed an increasing threat to the good eye resulting from infections in the injured one, the eye doctor replaced the source of the danger with an artificial eye.

That accident may have strengthened the tenderness underlying the love that the rest of us felt for the youngest member of the family. Fortunately, despite the trauma, Roger remained the happy, easy-going, good-natured child he had been from birth. The loss of vision in one eye didn't seem to diminish the activities of the otherwise healthy and vigorous boy. As the baby of our family grew into the kid brother, the pattern of his life, formed with his own circle of close friends, was not unlike what I've described about myself and Lew: school, homework, household chores, sports, hiking, fishing, kids' parties, and the rest.[23]

Like virtually every other boy in Skagway, Roger acquired a .22 rifle. Like the rest of us, he needed only one eye for aiming his rifle, and after some target practicing on tin cans over at the riverbed, he became a passably good shot. But it was obvious to everyone but Roger that he was far too young to accompany us on our hunting trips.

As he grew older our refusal to let him join us on these expeditions seemed to him more and more unjust. As kid brothers will do, this kid brother pestered his older brothers to take him along. When he was around ten and had finally pestered us to the limit, we gave in. "Alright! We'll take you when you're twelve!" Though I don't remember his response, I can imagine that he haggled a bit: "You mean in the fall just before my twelfth birthday or are you going to make me wait another year, until I'm almost thirteen?" Yes, Roger, we're going to make you wait until you're past your twelfth birthday, almost thirteen.

That time arrived in 1934. Shortly after the season for Rocky Mountain goats had opened in August and before Lew and I would head out to Seattle for another year at the University, the three brothers climbed the steep trail up 3,000 feet to Upper Lake Dewey and the log cabin that was open to anyone who might wish to use it.

❧

---

[23] In 1989 Roger wrote a narrative of some fifty pages, "My Life in Skagway, An Account of My Childhood in Skagway, Alaska," which, as I mentioned in my acknowledgements, I have found helpful in writing my own memoir.

Around four the next morning we rouse ourselves, cook a breakfast of bacon, eggs, and coffee, shoulder our rifles and packs—empty except for our lunches and therefore fully available for the goat quarters that we hope to carry back that evening—and head up toward a familiar slope on Lower Dewey Peak where we'd seen goats in previous years. A full moon, as I remember, is still in view. As dawn succeeds daylight and a bright sunny sky overtakes the dawn, we trudge on.

By ten we have reached a good stopping point. The ridge on which we've been hiking runs sharply downward for several hundred feet and ends in a narrow divide where the peak then begins its almost vertical rise. Four or five hundred yards directly across from us we can see the steep green meadow where we've sometimes spied goats in previous years. A few feet down the ridge on which we've been traveling we discover a narrow ledge where we can sit comfortably and view the distant meadow for signs of the elusive animal we're seeking.

We lean our rifles against the rise behind us, lay our packs alongside our rifles, and sit down to study the meadow with our single pair of field glasses.

Let me say a few words about our equipment. The field glasses (as we called them rather than "binoculars") are of World War I vintage and have been purchased from a surplus Army store in Pennsylvania. They're just adequate. The rifles that Lew and I carry, which were also surplus army equipment, are of even older vintage than the field glasses, for they're a legacy of the Spanish-American war when the infantry was equipped with the 30-40 Krag-Jorgensen, a rifle that holds six rounds and works by bolt-action.

Though I had always thought the Krag-Jorgenson was Danish, on one of our trips to Norway Ann and I visited the city in which the Krag-Jorgensen gun factory had been located. I then realized that it was actually Norwegian. The U.S. Army later replaced the 30-40 Krag with the Springfield 30 '05. As a left-hander who shot a rifle from his left shoulder, for me to cope with the right-handed bolt action of the 30/40 and the Springfield required some swift movements that right-handers—the privileged class—were spared. But I managed. In basic training, before the M1 had been issued to us and we were still using the Springfield on the firing range, I deftly concealed my maneuvering as a left-hander and thereby won my Expert Marksman badge.

Like other rifles of its day, the military 30-40 Krag had a very long barrel, much too long to lug through underbrush and up steep mountains.

So the surplus Army equipment firm in Pennsylvania converted it into a carbine by sawing a foot off the end the barrel and replacing the sight. When Lew and I tried out our new rifles we soon discovered that while his was pretty accurate, mine shot a foot or so under the bull's eye at a hundred yards and correspondingly more as the distance increased. So I learned to aim under the target by an amount that experience showed was about right—an allowance that in the local jargon we called "Kentucky Windage," a slander no doubt derived from the assumed unreliability of the rifles used by Kentucky and Tennessee mountaineers.

Roger's rifle is his .22, which as we all know is about big enough for a squirrel or a rabbit but probably wouldn't bring down a goat—much less a grizzly bear.

Which is exactly the animal that now stumbles upon us.

For some time, the three of us have been sitting on the ledge while we pass around the field glasses, stare across at the green meadow, and now and again carefully study a suspect bit of white that doesn't seem to move, as a feeding goat would, and, alas, on closer inspection proves to be nothing more than a whitish rock. Lew is seated on the extreme right end of our ledge, where it turns back and disappears around the low rise behind us. I sit a few feet to his left and Roger to my left.

Suddenly I hear Lew mutter, "Jesus Christ!"

I look toward him. Just beyond Lew, ambling toward us, is a bear. From its hump it's got to be a Grizzly!

The wind must be blowing in our direction, and the bear, we later surmise, hasn't smelled us.

The bear is as surprised as we are. It pauses, stares, not yet certain, it seems, of its next move.

Each of us whirls around to retrieve our rifles parked behind us.

For an instant, three lives hang in the balance: Lew's almost certainly, possibly Roger's and mine as well.

For whatever reason—our sudden movement, the glint of our rifles, a sudden surge of caution—the bear abruptly turns, flees, disappears around the bend of our ledge.

We jump up, swiftly climb the low rise behind us, and lo! the bear is running away from us. What a relief!

Suddenly we're transformed again into three mighty hunters. By God! we'll shoot that bear!

By now it must be over a hundred yards away and running fast. We lay down a barrage that includes bullets from Roger's less than lethal .22.

At around 200 yards the bear drops! It lies down, kicking feebly. We fire a few more rounds. The bear has stopped moving.

We approach cautiously.

The Grizzly bear is dead.

※

On examining it we confirm that it is indeed a Grizzly, and from its size and weight, which we estimate at over 200 pounds, we guess that it's probably about two years old.

Roger, who makes no claim to having brought down the bear, takes a photo of each of us in turn, kneeling alongside our Grizzly.

What are we to do with it? Well, skin it, obviously; pack out the skin; send the hide out on the next boat to Seattle for tanning. We'll then try to decide who gets to keep our bear rug. What a wonderful opportunity that bearskin rug will provide for bragging about our bear hunt. With the encouragement of the bear rug our story of "The Time We Shot the Grizzly Bear" will survive down the generations!

So we set to work skinning the Grizzly. It is now obvious, as indeed we had assumed all along, that the lethal shot must have entered the bear as it was running away from us.

About half way through, one of us raises a troublesome question: "Is there an open season on Grizzly bears?" If not, we're in trouble. If we return to town with the skin and assert our bragging rights among our friends, we'll have to report our bear to the game warden. But suppose there's no open season on grizzlies? Or suppose there is, but right now happens to be the closed season. What are we going to do?

Grizzly bears are famous for their unpredictability, which includes attacks that leave their human victims dead or badly injured. On at least one occasion that I can recall, two Indians from Carcross, a father and son, were brought down on the railroad to the hospital for Dad's surgery. They'd been picking blueberries, the father said, and as they rounded a patch of blueberry bushes they ran right into a mother Grizzly with a cub. She attacked, and by the time she had finished they were badly mauled, though not dead. They recovered, carrying with them throughout their lives, I imagine, some very bad scars—and a profound respect for Grizzly bears.

Lew with the Bear

Myself with the Bear

We've frequently read or heard about other attacks, some lethal.

So among Alaskans the Grizzly is not exactly viewed as a cuddly teddy bear. It's an animal to be respected for its ferocity, feared for its unpredictability, and avoided because of its lethality.

Our solution now becomes obvious. We'll report that we were attacked by the Grizzly and we killed it in self-defense. There are no witnesses to deny our story, it's highly plausible, and no one in Skagway, including the game warden, will challenge it.

The Mighty Hunters

We finish the skinning. Having heard somewhere that bear liver is the one edible part of the animal, I cut out a slice of the liver. As Lew and I take turns carrying the smelly hide, we return to the cabin. We nail the hide to an outer wall and Roger takes a photo of the two mighty hunters standing on each side of the bear hide.

As the liver sizzles in the frying pan on top of the cabin's stove, it yields a fishy aroma. Roger and Lew easily resist the temptation to give it a try. Since I'm the one who brought it back, I feel obliged to taste it. It's loathsome. I rush to the door and spit it out. Obviously our Grizzly had just ambled up the mountain after gorging on salmon in a stream down by the Bay. Next morning we head down to the town, where we let it be known that we'd killed a Grizzly bear in self-defense. No problem.

The following day, Lew and I head off for our jobs on the railroad section, while Roger takes on the bear-hide.

"Since Lew and Bob were working on the section at the time," Roger writes in his account[24], "I was assigned to the task of preparing the hide for shipment to a taxidermist in Seattle. I spent several days scraping the skin free of any vestige of meat and, after a heavy application of rock salt, we shipped it off on the next boat to Seattle. However, subsequently we were notified by the taxidermist that, due to the presence of parasites, the skin arrived in such poor condition that, without a substantial and expensive repair process, it was not practicable to proceed with the tanning. Needless to say, it was disappointing."

And who knows? Maybe he was lying, maybe he turned the hide into a handsome rug, and maybe he sold it for a pretty penny—maybe to a would-be hunter who maybe bragged thereafter about his bear hunt. Damn!

❧

At work the next day, Lew and I feel obliged, naturally to share with our comrades our great experience in shooting a Grizzly bear.

We had finished the morning's tasks and had about wrapped up our story of bringing down the bear, when, as we walked back to retrieve our lunch-buckets, Dean Story turned to Lew and asked, "Lew, everyone says grizzlies are hard to kill. When you brought it down, just where did you manage to hit your bear?"

Lew was by nature direct and honest, and not pausing to think about his answer, he described where the fatal bullet had entered.

"I'll be god-damned," said Dean without a pause, "that's the only time I've ever heard of a Grizzly bear attacking someone ass-end to."

He and our other fellow workers swore to keep our secret, and maybe they did.

---

[24] "My Life in Skagway," 1989, p. 40.

18. The Best Years of Their Lives

Beyond all doubt, the twenty-five years Mother and Dad spent in Skagway were the best of their lives.

They swiftly gained a circle of close friends and a warm acquaintance with virtually everyone in Skagway, of all ages. On her 90th birthday Mother recounted their life in Skagway with nostalgia: "There was never a dull moment, really. It was a very interesting life."

An avid and expert bridge player, Mother quickly acquired a circle of bridge-playing companions. One of her closest friends was "Dusty" Hannan, who had grown up in England, where she met and married her English husband (who hailed from Jamaica) and still retained the strong accents of her native England. As Mother explained:

> We called her Dusty because she was always saying, when we'd put down our bridge hand, "Well, that's not so dusty.'" [Mother and Dusty] used to go up to Carcross [in British Columbia] to play bridge with Mrs. Simmons and her daughter. There weren't any of the modern facilities in those days in Carcross. So when we had to go to the toilet, we had to go outdoors. Well, Dusty got a little tired of that. And so that time, after we'd had to use a four-pound coffee can, the next time we went, she said, "I'm going to take a little pot when I go." So we get on the train and go to Carcross with her holding her chamber pot.
>
> The Hannans had a cabin up at [the Portage], remember? We women used to go up there for two or three days and we'd play bridge. And I said to one of them, "I don't think I was built for sitting on a four gallon gasoline can for four hours." That's what I was sitting on. Things were kind of bare."
>
> *They not only played bridge.*
>
> You know, in Skagway, how we always played poker every Saturday night 'til 5.00 in the morning. *[RAD: "Every" is definitely an exaggeration.]*

138 THE BEST YEARS OF THEIR LIVES

Mother and Dad

At this point Roger intervenes. "That was penny-ante," he points out. "You couldn't lose that much money, though, could you?"

"Well," Mother responds, "I'll tell you, I always said, if I didn't have to pay your Dad's losses, I could have made quite a bit of money because I was lucky at poker and he wasn't."

I suspect that she was simply a shrewder player.

Much as she enjoyed bridge and poker, Mother's activities in Skagway went far beyond her card games. Among their good friends were some who enjoyed staging dinner parties for which every man donned his "best" suit (possibly, in fact, his only suit) and the women all wore long gowns. As a matter of course Mother and Dad were invited, and as best I could tell then or can now recall they greatly enjoyed them. However, Mother must have felt that her Iowa wardrobe was not quite up to the appropriate standards, so she opened an account with B. Altman's in New York City, where for decades she bought her gowns.

The only time she ever actually went in the store itself was during a trip to New York in 1940. The previous year, when New York City held its World Fair:

> Dad went back and I wouldn't go with him. I said, "If you don't go and ask for a vacation, I'll do it for you and I'll buy your ticket and I'll throw you on that ship. But I'm not going with you. You're going to have a good time with the boys." *["The boys" meaning Lew and me, of course; perhaps the best part of our good time together was attending the World Fair.]* So they did. So then Dad insisted that I go back in the Fall [1940]. Well, I had never been in New York alone before and I guess I went first to where you lived [New Haven] because you were with me. And you remember, you said, "Mother, I just hate to let you go to New York alone. You've never been there before." And I said, "Well, one city's about like another."

At my suggestion, on her arrival she called up two old friends of Mary's and mine from Mary's days with the International Ladies Garment Workers, Morton Wishengrad and Bill Gomberg.

> I guess you told me to call them and tell them what hotel I was at. So then they came down the next evening to take me to a show. And they said, "What did you do today, Mrs. Dahl?" And I said, 'Oh, I went down Fifth

Avenue, shopping along the way 'til I got to Altman's where I had a charge account." They said, "You've never been here before and you went down Fifth Avenue to 34th?" I said, "Well, yes. Every city is just a city." Come to find out, they'd never even been to Philadelphia." *[Laughter]*

As to the parties, I have no doubt that they were highly convivial. Before dinner and after, Scotch would be served, and perhaps a rum drink as well. Even during Prohibition, good Scotch and rum were not difficult to obtain in Skagway. They were legal in Whitehorse, and a friendly trainman would have no difficulty bringing back a bottle or two in the confident knowledge that the American custom agent was unlikely to search the luggage of a regular trainman and fellow townsman.

Mother came to enjoy a nip of Scotch. She learned to drink it straight; as Alaskans would say, you don't want to ruin good Scotch by adding water. Many years later she would tell about the time while she was flying from Seattle to New York on a visit to her sons when a flight attendant asked the little old white haired lady what she might like to drink, "Fruit juice? Ginger ale?" "No," Mother answered, "I'll have Scotch." "With soda, Ma'am?" "No," she replied to the startled attendant, "I always take mine straight."

Although cards and dinner parties were enjoyable diversions, they were only one part of Mother's life. She was active in the Eastern Star, the women's auxiliary of the Masonic lodge to which Dad belonged; in the affairs of the Presbyterian church, where she taught Sunday school for a time; and in school matters whenever parental participation was vital, at least during the dozen years that one or more her sons attended the public school.

But the activity in which she was most deeply involved was her family. She started her day by getting up in the morning to make breakfast for all of us before we headed off to school or, in summers, to work or, in Dad's case, to the hospital or to visit a patient. What's more, except during the later summers when Lew and I worked on the railroad section (when we each carried a well-packed metal lunch bucket and a thermos of coffee to the section of line on which we'd be working that morning) we all came back to the house for our lunch—which with three growing boys was a substantial meal—and around six or so we were ready for our big dinner.

She cooked and baked, she washed our clothes, she hung them out to dry, she brought them back in the house for ironing, folding, and putting away, she made the beds, she cleaned the house, sometimes with the help of Mrs. Couture. Though Lew, Roger, and I had our "chores"—carrying the dishes from the table to the kitchen after meals, stacking a dozen cords of firewood in the fall, splitting it for kindling, making the fire on fall and winter mornings, mowing the lawn in the summer, weeding the vegetable garden and flower bed—these were small tasks in comparison with hers.

I can't recall ever hearing her complain about her duties, which like many women she accepted as a part of her life.

Meanwhile, she came to know virtually every person in town, and they her. When a battalion of U. S. Army Engineers arrived in Skagway in 1942 to take over the running of the railroad, who was the obvious choice to head the U.S.O? Mother, naturally.

If a prize had been awarded to the most loved and admired woman in Skagway a quarter century after she had arrived in Skagway as a total stranger, I'm pretty certain it would have gone to my mother.

※

The men's prize would definitely have gone to Dad. He won the trust and confidence of whites and Indians alike—young, old, and in between. When they needed him, he came, day or night. Sometimes people who needed him for hurts that required more than a physician's usual remedies would turn to him for help in healing their invisible or unmentionable wounds. Probably more people shared their secrets with him than they did with their priest, Father Gallant, and their Presbyterian minister, Warren Griffiths. As Roger put it: "His role was far more than that of a doctor. He also played the part of veterinarian, village priest and confessor, and family counselor; invariably, he was the one who received a call from the battered wife whose husband had come home after his Saturday night binge."

He kept his confidences. Even at home, in our conversations at the dinner table or afterward in the living room or out on the porch on a summer's evening, he was highly discreet. He probably shared more of his professional secrets with mother than with Lew, Roger, and me, and she, too, was highly discreet. People knew they could trust him with their confessions.

People also became aware that he could be counted on to be there when they needed him. I have always remembered that tragic day when two of our Skagway youth drowned in Icy Lake. That small, lovely lake was appropriately named, for if you were foolish enough to jump in, as I did once or twice, its waters hit you with a brutal shock, which on the day of the drowning proved lethal. Although Dad walked to and from the hospital twice a day at a fair clip and was in good shape, he never developed a liking for our mountain trails. Dad remained a plainsman who enjoyed a brisk walk on flat land but not on the steep slopes of our nearby mountains. Yet on that sad day when word raced through the town that two of the three who had dived into the waters of Icy Lake had not resurfaced, Dad answered the call, even though the trail to Icy Lake was abrupt and exhausting.

As we futilely took turns trying to resuscitate the two victims by the first-aid method some of us had learned as Boy Scouts, I looked up and saw Dad walking toward us, still wearing his customary white shirt and blue suit, his vest unbuttoned, his tie awry, and more out of breath than I had ever seen him. He immediately took charge, and a few minutes later he announced that the two young men were dead. Nothing more could be done, except to undertake the sad burden of carrying the two bodies down the steep and stony trail.

As he always did, he came because he believed he was needed.

On rare occasions he even responded to calls from Chilkoot Barracks when the Army doctor happened to be away, even though the army post was fourteen miles to the south, near Haines, reachable only by boat on the often stormy Lynn Canal. Mother recalled the time when:

> ... they phoned up and they asked him to come down in the afternoon of this one day, and he went. As he was going out the door he came back and said, "You know where my insurance papers are, don't you?" That was so cheerful. I said, "Yes, I know." And then he went on. And the next morning, about 9:00, Father Gallant called me. He said, "Vera, do you know Doc has never gotten to Haines?" And I said, "What has happened?" He said, "We don't know, but what shall we do?" I said, "You'd better send somebody out to look for them." Well, they did, and they found them. They'd gotten into rough weather and the man who had taken him in his canoe [*boat?*] said, "I think we'd better hole up somewheres or we're going to the bottom, and do you need to get to Haines that much?" Dad said, "Not that much." So they sent out a hunting party and got them. That was a bad time."

Dad was as sociable as Mother. As I mentioned in an earlier chapter, on his way home from the hospital in the late afternoon, he would often drop in to Selmer's Barber Shop for a chat with the other men who, like him, had come there to share the gossip. Or walking home at the end of the day he would sometimes turn into Louie's Coffee Shop; after Prohibition ended and the coffee shop became Louie's Beer Parlor he might indulge himself in a drink of Scotch. On one occasion when he arrived home and joined Mother in the kitchen, he was visibly tipsy, much to the dismay of his two older sons, whose recriminations and Mother's tears thoroughly spoiled any pleasure he might have derived from what he had imbibed at Louie's. It was the only time I ever saw him so. Though he liked a drink now and again, he was fundamentally a temperate man.

He had one very close call that became known in our family as "The Time the Crazy Man Chased Dad down Broadway."

One morning several trainmen who were tending a string of freight cars next to a ship tied up at the dock caught sight of a seaman emerging stark naked on the ship's deck. The naked seaman walked over to the railing, climbed up it, jumped over to the dock, and walked swiftly in the direction of the trainmen. He grabbed the legs of one of them who was scrambling up the ladder of the freight car, pulled him down, and slammed him to the floor of the dock. What more he might have done was never revealed, for a nearby brakeman ran over and hit the seaman square on the head with his brake-stick. Bleeding profusely and unconscious, the seaman—hereafter in this narrative the Crazy Man—was trussed up, the U. S. Marshall, Louis Rapuzzi, was called, and soon thereafter the Marshall and the Crazy Man, now in handcuffs, appeared at the hospital, where Dad stitched up the man's head and sent them both on their way.

As Dad was walking down the wooden sidewalk on the west side of Broadway on his way home for lunch, he saw the Marshall and the Crazy Man walking up the sidewalk on the other side of the railroad tracks that ran down the middle of the street. The Marshall, it seems, was escorting the Crazy Man to lunch. Because the Crazy Man had become quiet and tranquil, the Marshall had temporarily removed his handcuffs.

Now free of his restraints, upon catching sight of Dad across the street the Crazy Man began walking swiftly toward him, crossed the tracks, and strode menacingly closer. (We later surmised that he must have viewed Dad as the person who that morning had caused him great pain and injury, perhaps even the one who had inflicted the damage to his head.) Not taking any chances, Dad began to walk swiftly down Broadway. The Crazy Man followed. Dad picked up his pace. The Crazy Man began closing in. Dad started running.

During his pre-med days many decades earlier, Dad had been on the University track team, running the hundred-yard dash. Although he had neglected to keep up his training during the intervening years, Dad now managed to stay ahead of the Crazy Man. Just barely. With the Crazy Man gaining rapidly, Dad reached the end of Broadway, where all that lay directly ahead were the beach and the Bay. No safe haven there. Dad turned sharply left, sped across the tracks to the sidewalk on the other side, and continued running, now heading north up Broadway.

As he raced along, directly ahead he saw someone standing on a ladder repainting the sign over the entrance to Louie's Beer Parlor. He recalled that the place had a rear exit. Perhaps he could elude his pursuer by running through the café and out the back door. Which he did. And so he escaped the Crazy Man.

But the sign painter did not. We called him Old Man Wallace. He was indeed old, thin, even frail. His presence on the ladder caught the attention of the Crazy Man, who pulled him off the ladder and began thwacking him to the ground. Meanwhile the Marshall, who had helplessly watched the Crazy Man chase Doctor Dahl down Broadway, up Broadway, and right past the Marshall, was galvanized into action. With the help of several men who had dashed out of the Beer Parlor, the Marshall managed to subdue the Crazy Man, though not without some damage to the Crazy Man's head that would require Dad's skills once again.

Meanwhile, Dad had arrived at the hospital, shaken and exhausted. He was soon confronted with two patients needing emergency care. One was Old Man Wallace, who had incurred many bruises and a sore back but no broken bones. The other was the Crazy Man, now manacled, whose head required new stitches.

The Crazy Man was returned to the town jail and sent Outside to a mental hospital on the next boat.

Old Man Wallace's injuries required Dad's attention for several months. Finally the time came when Dad could say to Old Man Wallace that he that he wouldn't have to come back another time.

As Old Man Wallace prepared to leave, he said: "Well, Doc, how much do I owe you?"

To which Dad replied: "Mr. Wallace, you don't owe me a goddamn thing. How much do *I* owe *you?*"

19. Town Characters: Comedy, Pathos...

Whether Skagway contained a greater percentage of eccentrics—town characters we called them—than many other small towns, I can't be certain. But I'm inclined to believe it did, because for many persons Skagway had been a catch basin at the end of their wanderings. For some it was a northerly terminus on the way to the gold fields in the Yukon that they never reached. For others it was a southerly terminus when, like thousands of others, they headed down from the Yukon. Whether they were headed up or back, in Skagway they might find work, if they chose, and shelter, if only a log cabin on the edge of town or a few hundred feet up on the slope of a mountain. And, if they wished, the company of other human beings—which not all of them did.

Like the extraordinary high and low tides that terminated at the end of Lynn Canal, the ebb and flow of human tides had deposited on Skagway's shores its own collector's items. Just as when you stroll along a beach you might stumble on all sorts of odd objects cast up by the sea, so too as you walked around Skagway you were likely to encounter one or more of the town characters.

I've already mentioned Harriet Pullen. Even more visible during the summer months was *Martin Itjen*.[25] I can't improve on Roger's recollection:

"Martin Itjen was the consummate con artist who made a very good living by providing a sightseeing service for the tourists during the summer. He must have been something of a mechanical genius, however, for he built and operated the "Skaguay Street Car" (his spelling)[26], a bus built

---

[25] For helping me to recall some of the names and details I am greatly indebted to Roger Dahl's "My Life in Skagway," pp. 8-12.

[26] Note by RD: Skaguay had been a common and perhaps prevalent spelling in earlier years.

atop a truck chassis and complete with all sorts of novelties to entice the tourists. On the front of the bus was a life-size statue of a bear which growled and pointed an arm, right or left, in the direction the bus was turning; on the back he had a life-size manikin of Soapy Smith which also had operating arms and head. The car was also equipped with a number of whistles, horns, and bells which Martin operated throughout his 25 cent two-hour tour of Skagway; during the tour he provided an interesting monologue about Skagway, Soapy Smith, and many of the other town characters, living and dead. At one time he drove the bus through many cities in the Lower 48 during which he met Mae West and invited her to come to work for him during the summer! Martin and his wife live in a small house built on top of the boat dock and none of us ever knew what he did all winter long. Perhaps that's when he counted the money he'd separated from the tourists the previous summer."[27]

Martin Itjen

Unlike Martin Itjen, we rarely see *Burro Creek Joe*, a hermit who lives alone some three miles across the bay where Burro Creek completes its

---
[27] P. 9.

wild dash down the steep granite slopes of Mount Harding and plunges into the sea.

Yet we might catch a distant view of Burro Creek Joe as he rows his skiff across the bay on one of his occasional trips into town to buy supplies, or catch a passing glimpse of him shopping for supplies in one of the stores.

If we venture across the bay to Burro Creek in the summer, for a picnic, perhaps, or to cast a trout line into the fast waters of the creek, we'll see more of him, in his own habitat. Like several of the other hermits I encounter in Skagway, Joe seems to welcome the occasional visitor, greeting you warmly in strongly accented English that still bears the traces of his French-Canadian origins. He looks to be around sixty, a tall, well-built man, with features partly concealed by his untrimmed beard that hint at an earlier well-formed, perhaps even handsome, head and face. The once natty dresser is now wearing a pair of dirty bib-overalls, a grimy shirt, and, covering his long and unkempt hair, a filthy cap. Joe is particularly proud of his "fly cap," as he calls it, which, he proudly tells you, is his very own creation. He made it, he tells you, out of a small flour sack that he has then covered with a greasy and rather smelly substance (bacon grease, bear grease, motor oil? I no longer remember). It's perfect, he says, for repelling flies and mosquitoes. It's effective also for keeping other human beings at a little distance.

I never saw him take off his fly cap, and I don't doubt his claim; like forested areas everywhere around Skagway, the woods surrounding Burro Creek were dense with mosquitoes and without some protection his head and face would have been a mass of bites.

The Skagway story about Burro Creek Joe runs like this: As a young man this friendly if now odoriferous and bedraggled hermit had been a town dandy, a gambler, one who attracted and was attracted to any good looking women around who might be friendly toward a professional gambler. Perhaps they were not the most "respectable" women in town, but no matter. With one, according to Skagway legend, he fell desperately in love. But alas! After a time she turned her affections to another man. Rejected in love, our town dandy left Skagway for a life of isolation from society, a hermit in Burro Creek.

How much of this story of love and rejection was truth and how much was fiction, I never knew. But I still see Joe, having spotted us perhaps as we pulled our boat onto the beach, walking down from his cabin to greet us in a very friendly fashion. Our response is as friendly as his welcome. Joe now turns loquacious. Hermit, yes. Vow of silence, no. In fact, he seems eager to talk—a characteristic I will observe in several other hermits, self-exiles who appear to long both for solitude and for human company.

If you let Joe talk on—he's not easy to stop—and he warms to the audience you provide, he invites you up to his cabin a hundred paces up the slope, where it sits right alongside the rushing waters of the Creek. Its interior is as dirty and unkempt as Joe himself. After sitting you down on a ramshackle chair—made, it appears, from an egg crate—the attentive host now offers you his *piece de resistance*: pancakes. Given the grimy surroundings, Joe's invitation is not only rather daunting but, since no pancakes are in evidence, somewhat mystifying.

But be not hasty. Joe now opens a small, battered steamer trunk and voila! It is filled with cooked pancakes! How long they have been stored in the trunk, will remain a mystery. Joe now picks out one for you—whether recently cooked or of an older vintage we have no way of knowing. He pours on a bit of blueberry syrup that he no doubt has made himself and passes it over to you, presented carefully in his dirty hands. What can you do? Eat it, of course. As you gulp it down, Joe looks on with pride.

On later visits to Burro Creek I become more adept at politely fending off his hospitality: "Thanks very much, I've just eaten." "Sorry, we must be getting back." Etc.

My lasting impression is that Joe was genuinely pleased with our company and his opportunity to be hospitable. So, I ask myself, was he lonely? Did he miss human company? Probably. Was he relieved when we finally shoved off and left Burro Creek entirely to him? I expect so.

But what went on in the mind of Burro Creek Joe, I have never fathomed.

❀

I became acquainted with *Herman Garmatz* when we occasionally worked alongside one another on the dock during the summer. I can't remember that he ever shared much with me about his life before Skagway, but perhaps I never probed, or if I did I may have probed too crudely.

Herman is a short, heavyset man with a large head and massive arms and legs. Like Joe, Herman speaks with a strong accent—whether German or Central European, Czech perhaps?—I may have never known. But Herman is unlike Joe in other respects. For one thing, Herman is fairly neat and tidy, and so too, I discover in time, is the interior of his cabin. For another, Herman lives within walking distance of the town, in a cabin standing alone in the woods several hundred feet up the steep slope of Dewey Mountain on the east side of town. Though his location gives Herman the isolation he wants, he can easily walk down the path to the town and back up to his cabin. Herman is unlike Joe in another way: he works at a job—longshoring. To be sure, it isn't exactly a steady job, for while tourist boats and freighters come frequently during the summer, their fortnightly visits during the rest of the year mean that Herman has little employment from September to June. Yet he manages to scrape by.

Herman obviously wants isolation. But like Joe he seems to like occasional visitors. One day when Lew and I are on the trail to Lower Lake Dewey, we catch a glimpse of Herman and we walk over to chat. After a time, he invites us to come into his cabin and share one of his delicacies. (What that was I no longer remember but I vaguely recollect a concoction created from the wild blue berries that flourished on a patch of bushes near his cabin.) The interior is neat and the receptacles from which we eat, or drink, his concoction seem clean enough.

That and other memories leave residue of a man who was both lonely for human contact and at the same time fearful and suspicious of what others might feel or do. Was his suspicion a bit paranoid? Perhaps. But if so, his hesitation about trusting other people will prove to be justified.

Perhaps too his vision of the future is different from Burro Creek Joe's.

For Herman is mining for gold not far from his house. With pick and shovel, over the years he's turned over a substantial amount of gravel and rock. But he seems to be confident that his persistence will finally yield a vein of gold or at least a nugget or two. As he mines for gold in his back yard on the rocky mountainside, perhaps he dreams of vast riches still to come—a dream that will last until some of the town's practical jokers put a cruel end to his hopes.

With his savings from his work at the docks he even buys a few sticks of dynamite from time to time. The noise of his blasting for gold arouses the interest of some of the folk in town. Among these are a few men who delight in practical jokes who create a "nugget" by covering a stone with copper paint. One day when Herman is down in town shopping for supplies, our practical jokers swiftly make their way to his most recent mining site and there they conceal the nugget under a layer of gravel.

Several days later Herman comes racing down into the town, shouting (as I later heard the story) "Eureka! Eureka! I've found gold at last!"

While his nugget is shipped off to Juneau for an assay, I imagine he must dream on. At last! At last! His hopes fulfilled! Riches! A new life for Herman Garmatz.

In due time, the results of the eagerly awaited assay arrive. He is crushed and humiliated. His deepest fears and suspicions about his fellow human beings are confirmed. He will become ever more of a recluse.

Yes, Skagway tolerates its town characters and is even rather fond of them. But in the end, town characters are also outsiders, and among some Skagwayites tolerance can turn to cruelty—unthinking cruelty, perhaps, but unthinking cruelty can still be devastating.

It must have been so for Herman Garmatz.

❈

We call him *Ol' Man Davis*. His claims to have fought in the Civil War are generally accepted, so when we first begin to encounter him he is probably in his mid-sixties or early seventies. He is still working on the railroad section, though by the time Lew and I begin our summers as gandy-dancers he will have retired.

Ol' Man Davis is notable for at least four things. First, he lives by himself, though unlike Burro Creek Joe and Herman Garmatz he frequently strolls around town. Second, he has a reputation for possessing unusual physical strength. Third, he never bathes. In fact, he hasn't bathed for many, many years because, as he is ready to tell anyone who is within range of his voice, bathing is harmful to the health. His superior strength and obvious robust good health provide him with all the solid empirical evidence he needs to refute any skeptic. Finally, and not surprisingly, he emits a prodigious B. O.

Because Ol' Man Davis is amiable and talkative, a chance encounter with him as he strolls about poses a strategic problem. How can you respond to him with courtesy and respect and at the same time remain safely out of range of his powerful though perhaps not altogether lethal emissions?

Because of an important characteristic of the weather in Skagway, you craft a strategy. In Tlingit, the word Skaguay means "home of the North wind," and much of the time the town is subject to north or south winds. The long fjord of the Lynn Canal and the continuing valley in which Skagway and the White Pass are located, together with the cold ocean water of the Bay, seem to generate unceasing air currents—either cold, dry winds that come barreling down from the north in the winter, or the warmer, wet winds that soar noisily up Lynn Canal and drop their rain or snow as they pass through. In Skagway we become so accustomed to the wind that, as some residents like to say, breezy or calm we walk bent forward as if we were heading into a wind.

So you evolve a double-barreled strategy. First, never go into a store, or any other enclosure, where Ol' Man Davis happens to be. Second, if at all possible get up-wind of him as soon as you can. The second can be tricky. If you see him walking down Broadway on your side of the street, should you cross over to the other side? No, that might be too obvious and thus too rude. So you edge out on the side walk and pass by him as quickly as possible. If for some reason you then want to chat, you're safely upwind.

How many people other than I pursued this wily strategy, and whether Ol' Man Davis ever detected it, I have no idea. No matter, he remained an amiable old character.

Finally even Ol' Man Davis could not prevent the inevitable. One cold morning a neighbor who kept an eye on his chimney noticed that no smoke was rising from it. A few moments later, Dad was called. Ol' Man Davis was being brought to the hospital. By the time Dad arrived, the odor informed him on walking in the door that Ol' Man Davis was already there. He was alive, a nurse said, but barely conscious.

"We must bathe him immediately," she said. That was the standard practice, and no doubt she was also considering how soiled she, the other nurses, the doctor, and the sheets would become as he was examined.

"No," said Dad. "Don't bathe him. If you do he'll die of shock."

The nurses assumed he must be joking. They gave him a bath.

He died in the tub.

When they told Dad, he said, "I told you not to bathe him because a bath would kill him."

In later years, I sometimes pressed Dad: When he gave his initial order and in his final comment to the nurses had he been really serious, or just joking? On the only occasion that I can now remember, he never gave me a straight answer.

20 .... AND TRAGEDY

I no longer remember just when Ed Gedney came to Skagway, but it must have been a few years after our own arrival—1928, say?

Ed Gedney was a remittance man. The term probably came to us in Skagway via White Horse, for it is an English usage that denotes an errant son of an upper class family whose behavior so threatens the family's good name that he is sent abroad—Canada, Australia, South Africa, India, perhaps—adequately endowed with a regular stipend to insure that he never returns.

Ed Gedney was Skagway's remittance man. He came from a wealthy New York family that supplied the funds to keep him away.

Ed Gedney was a drunk. He had been a drunk from boyhood on.

He was a tall and, despite the excessive alcohol, unusually handsome man, strong and athletic, with a rangy stride that enabled him to eat up the miles when he traveled through the woods.

Sober, he was exceptionally charming, intelligent, easy and amusing in conversation, and by no means unwilling to share tales of his wild escapades and the futile efforts of his family to overcome his addiction to alcohol. Because of his charm, he soon made some friends in Skagway, notably two of the most attractive younger couples in town, Jack and Bess Conway and Prosper Ganty and his wife. Jack and Pross, local boys by origin, were graduates of the University of Washington and about ten years older than Lew and I, who in our early teens looked upon these two witty, attractive, and sophisticated young men as models we aspired to imitate. The sober Ed Gedney soon won them as his friends.

Drunk, Ed Gedney was a staggering, falling-down disaster. You could understand why his family didn't want him around.

Jack and Pross and their wives were evidently willing to overlook his intermittent periods of drunkenness.

Ed Gedney also found acceptance in Dad and Mother, who, like Jack and Pross were delighted by his easy charm when he was sober, even if they were appalled by his behavior during his drunken episodes. Three encounters with Ed Gedney have stuck in my mind.

Two of them occurred on our glassed-in front porch, the largest room in the house, where we regularly gathered on summer evenings after dinner, when daylight dimmed but never fully vanished, and where we might read, talk, or simply gaze out upon the magnificent scenery that rose up to the sky—almost, it seemed, at our front door.

❁

I still remember those first evenings following my return home for the summer after nine months away in Seattle or New Haven, when I would gaze steadily upon Dewey Mountain, its familiar slopes and peaks, the deep green of the pines, spruces, and hemlocks blanketing the mountain up to the tree line at three thousand feet, the lighter green of the grassy slopes above, the creek and falls plunging down from Upper Lake Dewey, the massive dark granite of the peaks, here and there a patch of snow and ice persisting through the summer, and, I could easily imagine, on the green and grassy slopes below the peaks, Rocky Mountain goats might be feeding, tiny white spots against the green, too small for me to see from such a great distance; and if I turned to look across the bay at Mt. Harding and the nameless mountains lining Lynn Canal, I could see the enduring glaciers hugging the peaks.

Those moments filled me with a kind of bliss that I still feel, more faintly perhaps, when I ride up into the Bob Marshall Wilderness in Montana.

❁

One summer evening a few years after Ed Gedney arrived in Skagway he appeared at the door, perhaps to see Dad about something. Whatever the ostensible reason for his visit, he stayed on, chatting amiably, clearly in need of some sociability. What I remember most vividly is his description of the futile attempts by his family to cure him of his alcoholism. They sent him off to a number of private boarding schools, each one of which booted him out after some particularly outrageous episode of drinking. In desperation, his family also placed him in institutions that promised to cure his addiction. One, I recall, employed what today we would call, I suppose, aversive training: he would be encouraged to drink and drink until he was horribly sick, vomiting prodigiously, sick as the proverbial dog. Ed concluded his narrative with a touch of perverse pride that may have been a clue to his self-destructiveness by saying that as soon as he recovered he would get drunk again.

Not long after that evening, Ed built himself a cabin deep in the woods some miles from the town of Haines, fourteen miles to our south. Perhaps he was searching for a cure in solitude. He bought whatever supplies he needed in Haines and carried them on his back for the long and arduous trek to his cabin. And from time to time he would board the converted minesweeper that ran as a ferry between Skagway and Haines, the Fornance, for a visit in Skagway, seeing his friends the Conways and Gantys, and perhaps dropping in on the Dahls.

His hard and solitary life in the woods seem to have helped. So much so that one year he returned to his origins in New York, fell in love, and came back to Skagway with a bride, a woman of such charm and beauty that every male in Skagway who saw her must have found her attractive. So too did Ed's friends, the Conways, the Gantys, and the Dahls.

A woman obviously accustomed to comfort and urbanity, she adopted Ed's new pattern of life. She would hike with him from the cabin to Haines for supplies, load her share onto her backpack, and trudge off through the woods. If she failed to keep up with Ed's stride, some folks claimed, he would leave her behind to make her own way to the cabin. When they returned to Skagway to visit, as they did from time to time, she was even more ravishing; in her jeans, moccasins, and a beaded jacket made for her by a Tlingit woman, she might have stepped out of a Hollywood film. Whether other women envied her I can't say; but I can say with confidence that males found her adorable.

The romance lasted for some years. But it was contingent on one crucial factor: not money, comfort, a social life, amenities ... No, the contract, implicit or explicit, was that Ed would stay sober.

She lasted through periods when Ed fell off the wagon. Like many wives of alcoholics, perhaps she believed that with her companionship, love, and comfort, he would stay sober. I have no idea how many periods of Ed's drunkenness she endured, nor how many times she might have said, "One more time, Ed, and I'm leaving." Well, there was one more time ... and one more ... and ....

Finally, she gathered up her meager possessions and departed on the next boat to Seattle, where she took the train back to New York.

To my knowledge, no one bore her any hard feelings. On the contrary, my parents, like the Gantys and Conways, felt that out of her love for Ed, and her hopes, she had endured him beyond all reasonable limits.

The next visit of Ed Gedney that I recall occurred several years later. As before, he showed up while we were all sitting out on our enclosed porch quietly enjoying a pleasant summer evening. He wanted urgently to talk with Dad. Although we discreetly avoided listening in on a conversation that was clearly intended to be private, we could hear enough to know that it did not go well. I remember hearing my father say, "No, Ed, I can't do that. I'm sorry." After Ed left, crestfallen, Dad explained that Ed had begged him to write his beloved and assure her that Ed was no longer drinking. But as Dad well knew, Ed Gedney continued to have his drunken bouts, and Dad would not falsely testify otherwise.

❈

The last time I saw Ed Gedney was at a tawdry bar in Haines.

In those years, Haines was a run-down place of several hundred inhabitants, a disproportionate number of whom—so it seemed to us in Skagway—were drunks, shiftless ne'er-do-wells, demoralized Indians, and whores who plied their trade with the soldiers in the Army battalion stationed at Chilkoot Barracks a mile or so away. Some of us in Skagway contemptuously referred to Haines as "the ass-hole of Creation."

Years later, after the Alcan Highway was built with a terminus at Haines, and Skagway fell into its own slump following World War II, as I mentioned earlier, when Haines briefly became larger and more affluent than Skagway some of the folks there, I've been informed, got their revenge by applying that term to Skagway.

❈

Perhaps I should explain why I was in a tawdry bar in Haines.

It was during a summer when work at the docks was episodic, before I shifted from longshoring to steady work on the section gang. How old was I? Sixteen, seventeen, eighteen?

158 Town Characters: ... And Tragedy

Glacier Bay around 1933

Margery Glacier

A Coast and Geodetic Survey boat came to Skagway searching for two able-bodied seamen. It seems that two of their crew had jumped ship—in Haines or Juneau perhaps. The word got around that they needed two crewmembers for a trip to Glacier Bay and back, ten days, two weeks. My friend Wil Goding and I decided to apply. We may not have met all the qualifications for an "able bodied seaman," but we were able enough, familiar with the ways of the sea, willing to work, and they took us on.

It was a trip I'll never forget. To this day, when the need arises I still splice a rope in the way the bos'n taught me—simple, really, but satisfying when you've finished your loop, or spliced two ends together, or neatly finished off an end. (I admit of a prejudice: I enjoyed splicing rope made of hemp more than I do with the synthetics that have largely replaced it. Hemp, I gather, now has other uses.)

The Lynn Canal and Glacier Bay form a V that is a little more than 100 miles from the base to the ends of each of the two sides. At the north end of Lynn Canal Skagway sits at the top of the eastern side. Glacier Bay, on the other side of a mountain range, forms the western side of the V. The Canadian boundary cuts squarely across the northern tip of Glacier Bay.

When John Muir explored the area in the 1880s, we were told, the glacial ice extended almost to southern end of the Bay. From recent reports by fishermen and others, officials at the Survey believed that the retreat of the glacier had made most of the Bay accessible.

The purpose of the trip to Glacier Bay, we learned, was three-fold: One was to make soundings to prepare a chart for waters that had never been accurately sounded. To make the soundings, the Coast and Geodetic Survey had equipped our boat with a new-fangled invention from Britain that, we were told, was called SONAR. A second purpose was to survey and accurately locate the boundary between Alaska and Canada. Third, if the glacier at the head of the bay had retreated enough, we were to build a permanent boundary marker.

We reached the bay around midnight. I had been ordered to take the wheel—with the skipper by my shoulder keeping his eyes on the compass, the water, and the best available chart, outdated though it was.

In the summer's twilight the dark slopes of the mountains on each side of the bay loomed over us. More hazardous were the numerous objects poking up through the waters of the Bay. Were they reefs? Or were they big pieces of floating glacial ice? As it turned out, they seemed to be mainly the second, but they were hazardous nonetheless.

So we moved very slowly, at a few knots or sometimes even cutting the engines and drifting, or putting them in reverse to avoid the unknown menacing object dead ahead.

Finally, near the head of the Bay we anchored, and I took to my bunk.

On awakening in full daylight and climbing up to the deck, I gazed on an awesome sight. To the north, at the head of the Bay, I saw two gigantic glaciers, from which huge chunks of ice periodically broke loose and crashed down into the sea with a roar. On each side of the Bay, steep mountains loomed up. Below the granite at the peaks were ugly black slopes that looked as if they had been created by an enormous giant playing with mud. So swiftly had the glaciers moved back from the head of the Bay that the lateral glacial moraines left behind were still barren of trees—none of the rich green forests so characteristic of Alaska's southern and southeastern coasts. (Later, on our way out, the Swedish cook would say: "I think that after God had finished the world he had a huge piece of mud left over, and he just threw it down here.")

Although I never returned to Glacier Bay by water, some years ago Ann and I flew over Glacier Bay in a small plane that skimmed over the blue-green ice of the glaciers and the waters of the bay. During the intervening years the bleak, dark, mud-encrusted mountainsides had become covered with the dense green of pines, spruces, and hemlocks, and the bay was now a popular destination for tourists, who might have found my descriptions of its earlier condition totally unbelievable.

The tasks the Survey had assigned were all successfully completed. With the aid of our new-fangled Sonar, the depths of the Bay were accurately sounded. Using survey equipment that we lugged to the top of a mountain on the northwest side of the bay, the skipper was able to determine the boundary and to signal a crew member armed with field glasses down below to mark it with some flags. The next day we built a lumber frame which we filled with big rocks gathered from the beach. Our boundary marker was sturdy enough, we thought, to last for many years. (Not sturdy enough, though, to withstand the glacier, which perversely began to move down into the bay and in a few years buried our marker under a massive layer of ice. *Sic transit . . .*)

On our return, the night before we were to head up to Skagway, we put into the harbor at Haines.

Along with other members of the crew, Wil and I went ashore and wandered into the only place where anything was going on, a dimly lit, run down bar. While we were sipping our beer we noticed a derelict at the far end of the bar, already, it appeared, half drunk. With a start I suddenly recognized the man as Ed Gedney.

I introduced myself—"Doc Dahl's boy, Bob, and my friend Wil Goding, from Skagway." For Ed Gedney, the words "Doc Dahl" were a talisman. He greeted us as friends, and after another beer or two he insisted what we come up to his room for a drink of good Scotch whiskey. Above the bar, it seems, were a few rented rooms, one of which was Ed Gedney's. It was about eight-by-twelve feet, and, like Ed, badly run down, not much in it but a cot and a beat-up old chair or two. Ed brought out his quart of White Horse and poured Wil and me each a drink in shot glasses that looked less than clean.

What we talked about while we downed our whisky I no longer remember. Wil and I left as soon as we could.

We said good by to Ed Gedney and hurried back to the boat.

On returning home from college a year later, I learned from Dad that Ed Gedney was dead. He had died in his soiled bed, in his unkempt room, above the tawdry bar, in the asshole of creation.

21. Outcasts in Their Own Land

Fifteen thousand years ago or more their ancestors began crossing over the ice that then briefly bridged the Bering Sea. They were the first of their species—our species—to occupy the virgin land that settlers who arrived long after would call the New World. Some groups remained in the Arctic regions, others settled inland, or when they reached the flatter areas further east chose to move south. Some kept going—and going—and going, perhaps no more than a few miles a year, until they reached the extreme southern tip of the Western Hemisphere. Others remained with the seas and paddled small craft down the coast, maybe settling down along the way among the countless islands and harbors, or like their inland cousins, moving on, and on, and on, until they too reached the very end of the vast land.

The groups became different tribes, with different languages, cultures, myths, organization. Some tribes depended primarily on hunting for their food, some on fishing, and some, like the Inuit in the Arctic regions, united both hunting and fishing as they searched the icy seas for the whale and the seal. Most tribes foraged. Some developed the arts of agriculture—cultivating corn, perhaps. The people in the various

Tlingit Carved Wood Figures

tribes inherited or developed different physical characteristics: the short, squat frames of the Inuit in the far north and among the Indians along the northwest Pacific coast were distinguishable from the tall and long-boned members of some tribes in the flatlands . . . .

The people who called themselves Tlingits or Tlinkits (or as we whites called them in Skagway, Klinkits) settled the islands, bays, and river mouths of the long inlet that ran up from the Pacific and to which some millennia later whites would attach the name Lynn Canal. The coastal climate was comparatively mild, the seas and rivers provided an abundant supply of fish—salmon, halibut, cod, huge runs of the small, oil-rich euligan (which we whites called "hooligan"). In the fall, the spawning salmon often ran up the rivers so densely that they formed an almost solid mass from one side to the other; and the euligan could be scooped up by the hundreds in nets or buckets.

Three brothers, headmen of the Chilkat Tlingit, Alaska 1907

The Tlingits developed a rich and complex culture. To describe it adequately would take me far beyond my knowledge and my intentions here, but a few examples may serve.

If you've ever seen a Tlingit blanket, perhaps on a visit to the Metropolitan Museum of Natural History in New York, you'll appreciate the Tlingit sense of artistry, which may also be seen in their exquisite carvings and the decorations on their moccasins and leather jackets. (By my time these were made mainly to sell to tourists, though I bought a pair of moccasins from Maggie Kadanaha that I sometimes wore when I hiked along the trails on lower AB Mountain imagining myself to be a white Leatherstocking.) Their totem poles are famously symbolic—in ways I've never fully understood.

Tlingit social organization was complex. All the Tlingits were grouped into four main tribes bearing a name that was also attached to the river or locale where they were mainly situated: Chilkat, Sitka, Stikine, Yakutat. The name of the tribe around Skagway and the corresponding river located a dozen miles south of Skagway was Chilkat. In addition to membership in the tribe, every Tlingit also belonged to one of two divisions or totems, the Ravens and the Wolves (in some villages, Eagles), within which marriage was strictly forbidden: a Raven was required to marry a Wolf, never another Raven, no matter where or how distant the village of the marriage partner.[28] Every Tlingit was also born into a specific clan with "a name denoting its place of origin, a story of its genesis, a history of its migrations."[29]

❈

The earliest European intruders were the Russians. In 1728 Vitus Bering, a Dane, (ah, those Vikings!) sailed east from Siberia in the service of Peter the Great and, like those who had arrived thousands of years earlier, discovered a vast continent of islands, mountains, glaciers, rivers, and potential treasures. In 1741, at the behest of the Empress Anna, Bering further explored the lengthy coast and learned about an animal whose pelt would fetch an astronomical price in the Chinese fur market in Canton: the

---

[28] Edward Sapir, "The Social Oranization of the West Coast Tribes," in Tom McFeat, *Indians of the North Pacific Coast* (Ottawa: Carleton University Press, 1989: 28-48: pp. 40-41

[29] Kalervo Oberg, "Crime and Punishment in Tlingit Society" *ibid.*, 209-222, p. 209.

sea otter. Though Bering died in a shipwreck on his return, the lure of the sea otter stimulated further exploration, during which the Russians also found still more treasures in the fur seals and blue foxes. Hunting these animals for their furs, the Russians quickly over-ran the Aleutians and Kodiak Island, leaving death, disease, and slavery in their wake.

They didn't stop there. By the end of the century a Russian trading company in the service of the Czar had gained such an extensive foothold that it moved its headquarters all the way down to a far southeastern outpost near the present—day town of Sitka—which, as its inhabitants and thousands of tourists can testify, still bears silent witness to the Russian occupation in its churches and other buildings.

Soon, of course, the Russians found themselves engaged in competition with other Europeans, British, Spanish, French. Then another emerging power, one closer at hand, finally got into the act—decisively. The American purchase of Alaska from the Russians in 1867 for 7.2 million dollars (as we learned in grade school) ended the competition among the Great Powers for Alaska and its riches. Henceforth Alaska was American—western American, frontier American, remote from the territory of the United States, yet definitely American.[30]

As with native peoples everywhere, the "guns, germs, and steel" of the whites devastated the Tlingits.[31]

❈

Of the five hundred persons who lived in Skagway, perhaps a hundred were Tlingits. By the time we arrived in Skagway and throughout my years

---

[30] When I was growing up it was still a Territory, not a state. The Territory of Alaska was entitled to one delegate to the U. S. House of Representatives, without a vote. In 1958 Alaska ceased to be a mere territory and became the 50th state. Wil Goding, the boyhood chum of Lew's and mine mentioned in the last chapter, became the administrative assistant to Alaska's delegate to Congress, Bob Bartlett, where he and the delegate worked to gain statehood for Alaska. Following statehood, Wil continued in his post when Bartlett became one of the first two Senators from Alaska. After Wil moved to the Department of Interior and later became High Commissioner to the Trust Territories of the Pacific, his sister, Margery, took his post in Bartlett's office, where she remained until her death.

[31] See Jared Diamond, *Guns, Germs, and Steel, The Fate of Human Societies* (New York: W.W. Norton, 1999).

there they were outcasts in their own land—or better, outcastes. For without excess exaggeration, one might say that they formed a caste—not, to be sure, the Untouchables of India yet a visibly lower caste. As in the other predominantly white towns of Alaska, the residents of Skagway occupied one of two castes: all whites were automatically assigned to the superior caste, all Indians to the lower caste.[32]

Yet that two-caste system was more porous, less strictly bounded, than the classical caste system of Hinduism, or that of the American South during and after slavery. By comparison with what I'll call the *hard* caste systems of Hinduism and, until recently, the American South, a better term for what existed in Skagway would be a *soft* caste system.

❀

Although the unstated rules of the soft caste system did not, to my knowledge, require segregated neighborhoods, most of Skagway's Indians lived in one of two small neighborhoods, one composed of several decrepit houses down near the dock; in the other, on the east side of the town, near the Skagway river, the houses were of somewhat better quality.

Among the softer aspects of our two caste system in Skagway was school attendance. From first grade through high school we all went to the same school, took the same classes, had the same teachers, sat alongside one another.[33] The boys played team sports together, basketball, hockey, baseball. Maybe it helped that our numbers were so small; as I've mentioned, it was a challenge to put two boys' basketball teams together,

---

[32] I use the term Indian or American Indian rather than the more politically correct term Native American or the Canadian First Americans because in my experience the term Indian is actually preferred to these by our native peoples.

[33] That we attended the same school may well have been a result of the fact that given the small number of pupils the town couldn't afford a second public school. In some larger towns like Juneau, separate schools did exist. I owe this fairly recent information to my friend Tom Stewart, who grew up in Juneau, whom Lew and I first came to know on shipboard when we traveled to and from the U. of W., and later when Tom went to the Yale Law School. Tom practiced law in Juneau, was appointed to a judgeship, and retired to his Juneau, where Ann and I have seen him on our visits to Alaska as well as at Mory's when Tom has been in New Haven for his law school reunions.

not to mention three boys' hockey teams. Anyway, in team sports we were elbow-to-elbow, shoulder-to-shoulder. After basketball or hockey we all took our showers in the decrepit locker room of the WP & YR athletic club with all the usual camaraderie, joking, and towel-snapping at naked male bodies.

※

Indians were welcomed in the two churches, Catholic and Presbyterian, and some chose to attend the church of their choice quite regularly. The shops and stores were accessible to whites and Indians alike. Both attended Skagway's one movie theatre, run by the Tropea family who owned the grocery store; but—evidence of the soft caste system?—Indians usually sat upstairs in the little balcony.

If they chose, which they rarely did, they could eat at one of the small number of places that served meals. An incident at the Golden Gate Café illustrates both aspects of the soft caste system, which though porous cold be exclusionary. One June after I returned from college I learned that during the winter a sign had appeared on the door of the Café: "No natives served here." The sign provoked immediate protests, from Dad, I believe, among others. The sign came down the next day.

That egregious declaration had over-stepped a boundary—or, more accurately, it had built a fence along what had been an invisible line that might be crossed and sometimes was.

The American melting pot has rarely produced immediate assimilation, and denigrating labels have usually been applied to members of ethnic groups that others view as outsiders—Squareheads, Hunkies, Dagos, Spics, Chinks, Japs, Niggers . . . .

In keeping with this ugly practice, among whites in Skagway and elsewhere in Alaska a derogatory term for Indians was "Siwash." How and where the word originated I've never known, though I've sometimes wondered if it might have been a corruption of "Salish," the name of the Pacific Coast tribe that Lewis and Clark encountered during their disagreeable winter of 1805-5 that they spent at the mouth of the Columbia.

Whatever its origins, Tlingits regarded "Siwash" as insulting and detested it. Although to the best of my memory it was rarely spoken in their presence, I sometimes heard it among white males, usually preceded by a pejorative word like "dirty" or "lazy."

Although whites and Indians worked alongside one another on the dock and railroad sections, whether because of lack of education, or discrimination, or, probably, both, to the best of my memory no Tlingit held a white collar job in the WP & YR office, or a skilled job at the railroad shops, or worked as a conductor, brakeman, locomotive engineer, fireman, or trainman.

If the soft caste boundaries allowed friendship in school, at work, even in hunting and fishing, under the unwritten rules friendships with Indians ended at the front door. None of the Indians in my age group was ever invited to our house for dinner. Neither, of course, were lots of other Skagway people who didn't happen to be among the close friends of Mother and Dad, or Lew, Roger, and me. Although the boundary of the soft caste system coincided with the customary distinction in social relationships between close friends and others, unlike the usual friendships that tend to be somewhat open and subject to change, during my time in Skagway the social boundary between Indians and whites was more impermeable. Indian boys and girls were never invited to the parties that we white adolescents held for our friends; nor, of course, would they be asked to join the frequent dinners and parties among the adults. To the town dances of the fall and winter months—when, as with some exaggeration, we might put it the next day, "The whole town turned out"—Skagway's native people did not come. Nor, I think, would they have been welcome.

If sociability stopped at front doors, so did courtship and marriage. For a man to court a Tlingit woman was to risk almost certain ostracism by whites—quite possibly without his gaining acceptance among the Tlingits themselves. The taboo forbidding marriage was rarely violated. A man who did—and almost certainly it would be a white man marrying an Indian woman—automatically acquired the epithet of "squaw man." His children would be "half-breeds," fully accepted neither by whites nor, on the testimony of one I knew, by the Tlingits.

❀

The people in Skagway were as kind, as considerate, as generous, and when help was needed as helpful as any people I've encountered elsewhere, maybe even a good bit more. Their basic decency sometimes overcame their prejudices. So it was in the case of the girl I'll call Amy.[34]

Amy's father was white, her mother was Indian. Like others of her age, Amy attended school and as far as I know she was treated well by her fellow students and teachers.

Of Amy's mother I know almost nothing, though I vaguely I recall a timid, self-effacing, almost invisible woman who rarely strayed far from her house, and then only briefly, to buy groceries or what not.

At work on the docks I had sometimes encountered her father. I'll call him Jake. Jake was a broad-shouldered, strongly built, rather handsome man with few if any other redeeming qualities. He possessed a short and violent temper and he was loud-mouthed, a liar, and a braggart. My guess is that he had few friends, either among whites or Indians.

Late one night after Dad and Mother had gone to bed, they were awakened by the insisting ringing of the telephone. An emergency. The caller was one of the nurses at the hospital: Doctor Dahl, Please come at once, a young girl is about to have a baby.

It was Amy, who had been brought to the hospital by her mother at the last moment, when family disgrace could no longer be avoided.

Whether Dad reached the hospital in time to make the delivery, or a nurse took over, I don't know. No matter. A full term baby boy arrived in healthy condition. The fourteen-year-old mother was also fine, or at least as well as could be expected.

Amy and her mother soon revealed the name of the father. It was Jake. Both Amy and her mother had been too terrified of him to let anyone know that for several years Jake had repeatedly raped his daughter. (How Amy's pregnancy was concealed from her friends and classmates, I don't know). Now that dreadful fact could no longer be concealed. Fearing that Jake would inflict a brutal and even deadly retribution on Amy, her mother, and the infant, Dad called the Town Marshall, who immediately took Jake into custody.

A trial was held before a jury of Jake's fellow citizens who convicted him of rape. The judge sentenced him to a lengthy prison term, which

---

[34] Amy was considerably younger than I, and the account I'm about to narrate comes mostly from my parents and Roger.

because of Alaska's territorial status would be served a thousand miles away in a federal penitentiary.

After Amy had recovered and had nursed the baby until he could be taken to his adoptive parents outside Skagway, she returned to school. Beyond the school grounds, most people in Skagway, touched by what she had gone through, also treated her warmly.

Would the white residents of Skagway have treated Amy with less compassion if the father had been an Indian?

I'm inclined to believe that their fundamental decency would have impelled them across the implicit boundary and they would have responded in pretty much the same way. But I can't be certain.

❀

I've already mentioned Paul Wilson. The friendship we developed with Paul may help to illuminate the porous quality of Skagway's soft caste system. One August as Paul, Lew, and I worked away on the section we talked about hunting. Lew and I described the high valley hugged by steep cliffs and peaks where we had hunted and where the events recounted in Chapter 16 occurred.

Paul showed an interest, we invited him to go with us, and he accepted. So one long weekend the three of us climbed the steep mountain to our "secret" valley, stowed our food and blankets near the gushing stream that ran through it, and set out in search of the elusive goat. Paul chose to go off on his own, while Lew and I headed toward an area of cliffs and peaks where our previous experience suggested that some mountain goats might be munching away on a grassy slope. And so, as it turned out, they were. We were lucky, though the two goats we shot were not, and in late afternoon we made our way back to our campsite, each carrying a butchered goat and its hide in our pack.

Paul had not yet returned. We started a fire, fried up some bacon, made coffee with the clear water of the nearby stream, ate our bacon and hardtack, drank our coffee. No Paul. The light of late summer grew dim, then nearly dark. Still no Paul. We began to worry. Finally, to our relief we heard him approaching, and soon he emerged in the dim light.

Paul hadn't seen a single goat.

The next day we return to Skagway, Paul to his family and the following day to his fellow Gandhi-dancers on the railroad section.

In that experience can we detect faint traces of the soft caste system at work? We hunted together, we shared our food and our fire, we talked and laughed and kidded as friends and companions, we rolled up in our blankets next to one another and slept under the starry night. Yet on his returning home, Paul would rejoin his subordinate caste and we our dominant caste.

When friends and family inquired about the hunt, as surely they did, I can imagine how Paul might have felt. The Tlingit Indian whose ancestors had survived in these parts for thousands of years through their skills in hunting and fishing had been skunked by his two young white friends, interlopers in his own land.

Years later I sometimes found myself wishing that it had turned out the other way around: that Paul had shot a goat and we returned with empty packs. Or better yet, if all three of us had each shot a goat.

Yet even if luck or fate had written this happy ending to our hunt, once we returned to Skagway, Lew, Paul, and I would still have taken our assigned places in the soft caste system.

22. WE LEAVE

At the summer's end in 1938, as usual Lew and I boarded the boat for Seattle. But unlike our previous departures this time we all knew—Mother, Dad, Lew, Roger, and I—that in the summers to come Lew would no longer return to Skagway. He would graduate from medical school the following June and begin his internship, at the end of which, as we all took for granted, he would undertake a residency in internal medicine.

Our family life in Skagway was coming to a close.

Still, we assumed that in 1939 I would spend one last summer there, living at home, of course, and working as a section hand. I would then return to Yale to write my dissertation, and, we all hoped and even took for granted, receive my Ph. D. in June, 1940, and then take on a full time job—probably in Washington, D. C. working, so I hoped at least, in a New Deal agency.

What we didn't foresee was that, like Lew, I too had just finished my last full summer in Skagway.

During the previous academic year, 1937-38, which I had spent in Washington as in intern at the National Labor Relations Board, I had fallen in love with a fellow intern, Mary Bartlett, a recent graduate of Wellesley who hailed from Providence. After her internship she worked for a year as the social director of Local 91 of the International Ladies Garment Workers Union in New York City, and then moved to Providence to head the newly created Division of Women and Children of the State of Rhode Island. By the fall of 1939 she was living at home with her parents and her beloved Dora, who as cook, housekeeper, and baby sitter had been for Mary a second mother—sometimes, in Mary's affections, a first.

Her father served as treasurer in the Builders' Iron Foundry, a firm that had been created in mid-nineteenth century by his grandfather and an ancestor of the current head, Henry Chafee (whose son and grandson, incidentally, would later serve in the U. S. Senate).

After I returned to Yale at the end of that summer of 1938, Mary and I saw one another every other weekend or so, either in New Haven or Providence. On one of my visits to Providence her father raised the possibility of my working the next summer as a laborer in the foundry. Since the pay was about the same as on my section job in Skagway, I could not have considered it if her parents had not also invited me to live in their house on Rochambeau Avenue. After thinking it over, I agreed.

So instead of returning to Skagway for the summer of 1939, I went to Providence and worked at the foundry—a job, I discovered, that was no harder than longshoring or the section, perhaps less so, but far dirtier and more boring.

I lived in the Bartlett home.

By the end of the summer, to no one's great surprise I had proposed to Mary and she had accepted. On the assumption that I would finish my dissertation in time to receive the degree in June (an outrageously optimistic assumption, as I would learn in my later academic life when a dissertation standardly took two or three years, sometimes more) we agreed that we would be married in June a day or so after the Ph. D. ceremonies at Yale. And so it turned out.

Right after the wedding, with the reception still at full tilt, we headed west in Mary's two-door Plymouth, camped out along the way, boarded the boat to Alaska in Seattle, and spent three weeks in Skagway. There we stayed in a small cabin a brief walk from home that was rented to us by the owner—who was none other than my sixth grade teacher, Miss Gaffey. (To her pleasure and mine, I now addressed her as Lotte, and the "Robert" of earlier years had at last become "Bob").

After three lovely and unforgettable weeks, we boarded a ship bound for Seattle, where we began a leisurely trek to Washington, D. C. in the Plymouth. There our new life began.

As Mary and I waved good-bye at the dock, we could not know that she would never return to Skagway, nor that it would be thirty-one years before I would see the town again.

❀

Lew would return briefly in 1945. After the end of his military service in the Pacific as a physician in the Army Medical Corps and before he resumed his long-interrupted residency at the Massachusetts General Hospital in Boston, he made a brief visit to see Mother and Dad.

Roger would not come back to Skagway until 1947. Following his discharge from the Army in December, 1945, he returned to Seattle with Irene to complete his degree at the University of Washington. Two years later in the summer of 1947 he took a vacation from his course work and, accompanied by Irene, once again took the boat up to Skagway, where they spent the summer. Unlike Lew and me, however, Roger would retain a close connection with Alaska for many years. Because of his duties with Wien Airlines he was to spend much of his time in the State's main boomtown, Anchorage (where any features of a small Alaskan town that it might once have shared with Skagway were—except for its magnificent setting—rapidly vanishing).

❀

Dad and Mother left Skagway in 1950.

Even though Dad had finally bought a car, which saved him the twice-daily walk to and from the hospital during bad weather, perhaps he had begun to feel that the demands on his time and energies were becoming more than he continued to find satisfying.

Their sons and their families were scattered—Roger to Seattle, Lew to New York City and Long Island, I to New Haven.

The town had changed. With the end of the War, the Army battalion was withdrawn. The USO was disbanded. Competition from truck traffic on the Alcan Highway had drastically reduced the freight carried on the White Pass Railroad, along with its profitability and its ability or willingness to sustain the quality of medical care it had hitherto been able to provide its employees. Many of the buildings that had contained Skagway's shops and stores were decaying or empty. To walk up Broadway was to walk, it seemed, through a dying town.

Some of their friends had died; others had left; others would soon depart.

Perhaps they began to feel that the Skagway they had so much loved was disappearing—in large part had already disappeared.

Then came an event that precipitated their departure. Years later, Mother recalled that day.

"I remember one Sunday," she said, "that Dad stayed home all day, didn't go to the hospital, and one of the longshoremen came about 4:00 in the afternoon, and I went to the door and he came into the hallway and wanted Doctor. He said to Dad, 'What are you doing, Doc, home on Sunday afternoon?'"

"And I was mad. I said, 'This is the first Sunday in a year that he has been able to be at home.'

'Oh,' he said, 'Mrs. Dahl, I didn't mean it that way.'

"He was ashamed.

"But that's how Lew and I persuaded Dad it was time to leave."

By then Dad had reached the age of 65, which would allow him to retire and begin drawing on his Railroad Retirement pension. When they announced Dad's imminent retirement and departure, the town virtually went into mourning.

The people of Skagway turned their sadness into the greatest public display of affection and esteem that the town had ever witnessed—more, indeed, than most small towns have ever witnessed.

A week or so before the day of their departure, all those who knew and esteemed them—most of the town—gathered at the school for a farewell ceremony. With Mother and Dad seated on the stage of the school auditorium, a parade across the stage began that was made up of every person living still in Skagway whom Dad had delivered during his quarter century there. At the head of the parade were the most recent arrivals, cradled in the arms of a parent. They were followed by "Dr. Dahl's babies" in order of age, ending with the oldest, who had arrived during his first years. Several of these, in fact, had already been at the head of the parade, carrying their own newly born infants. Each of Dad's "babies" crossed the stage to where Dad stood and took his hand in theirs.

Skagway's aging artist and illustrator Vic Sparks later composed an affectionate cartoon of their departure, which is reproduced on the following page.

Best Wishes from Skagway

    The cartoon is followed by signatures by their fellow townspeople, many of whom I can readily recall from my own time there: Jeanette Hillery, Eddie Hestness, Chris Larsen, Mayme K. Gault, Cye Richter, Art Nelson, Bill Dewar, Dorothy Dewar, Jack Lee, Bill Feero, Bob Feero, Barbara Kalen, Jack Kirmse, Lotte Gaffe, George and Edna Rapuzzi....

    In due time, the old hospital building was torn town and replaced by a new and well-equipped clinic where medical needs were met for some years by a physician and later by a a nurse practitioner.

    The new facility was named The Dahl Memorial Clinic.

    The residents who still remember Dr. Peter I. Dahl have steadily declined in number, and one day not far off none will remain. Yet the clinic will stand as a memorial to a physician who lived up to the highest standards of his ancient calling and while doing so gained, with his beloved wife, the abiding affection and respect of all who knew them.

After The Gold Rush 177

❈

July, 1940 to August, 1971. Thirty-one years.

I return to Skagway with Kit, fourteen, as my companion. Mary had died the previous summer. A trip to Alaska, I have come to think, might help to diminish our deep sadness and enduring grief. For Kit it will be a new world, unlike anything he has ever seen. For me the huge empty spaces of my life might begin to be replenished with some of the joy and delight in existence that I had experienced for most of my life.

We spend a week in and around Skagway. Lew and Roger arrive to join us in fishing for grayling at the Portage. As in our earlier days, we stay at Ken Hannan's cabin forty miles up the White Pass railroad in British Columbia near the tumultuous headwaters of the Yukon River.

Kit and I then visit parts of Alaska that I had never seen: to Fairbanks by air; a flight past the Wrangell Mountains for a night and day at Point Barrow; back down to Fairbanks and on to McKinley National Park and views of its animals and that magnificent Wonder of the World, Mount McKinley, soon to become Denali; aboard the Alaska railroad to Anchorage, where we join my old boyhood friend, Rod Johnston, his wife Mil, and members of the extensive Johnston family I had known in Skagway; a flight out to the Bering Sea with Rod and inland to a fishing camp on a wild river; our return to Anchorage and finally a flight out to Seattle and on to New Haven.

The trip was a memorable return to Alaska, and for me it helped, I think, to begin the healing.

❈

Accompanied by Ann, I came back to Skagway several times later. The first time was in August 1977. Taking advantage of an invitation from the International House of Japan to give some lectures, we traveled up to Skagway by way of the Inside Passage, which had retained all its glorious scenery.

Marilyn, Lew's widow, had arrived a few days earlier with their three daughters and had already made the arduous climb to Upper Lake Dewey to scatter Lew's ashes over the terrain that he had known so well and loved so deeply.

A few days later we all took the railroad to the Portage, where the train made a special stop to drop us off at "Ken Hannan's cabin," which we still called it though it was now the property of the White Pass Railroad. There we spent three glorious days fishing for grayling.

I returned a second time with Ann in 1987 before traveling on to Anchorage, where I was to receive an honorary degree. My last visit to Skagway, accompanied again by Ann, came near the end of a Yale Alumni cruise in 1998.

Each time, Skagway had changed. In 1977 it was so much more bedraggled and run down than I remembered it that I insistently repeated to Ann that "This is not the way it was when I was growing up." Of course, nothing ever is. But Skagway really was run down.

Ten years later it had been so much spruced up by the Park Service that it was probably in even better shape than it had been in those good ol' days.

In 1998, a Yale Alumni Cruise gave us a chance to view great stretches of incredible beauty in that vast land, from the Tanana River north of Fairbanks to the Inside Passage in Southeastern Alaska.

Near the end of the cruise, our ship stops for a day in Skagway. The morning we arrive, Ann and I take the tourist train to the Summit, at the Canadian boundary twenty miles up the White Pass and the terminus for a railroad that now hauls only tourists. Like the other tourists, we ride back down to Skagway on a bus. The views are still as magnificent, as breath taking, as lovely as they had ever been.

And there is a touching reminder of the Skagway that was Dad's and Mother's. Ann and I are standing on the platform of the rear car, absorbed in the beautiful scenery on every side, when a trainman joins us. After confirming that I am Dr. Dahl's son, his first words are, "Your Dad delivered me." He then speaks with great warmth about Dad. He appears to be around fifty, from which I conclude that he must have been among the last of Dad's Skagway "babies."

That afternoon, Ann and I take a walk up Broadway. Keller's Drug Store, I see, has become Keller's Trading Post. Richter's Jewelry and Curio shop remains. But both, I learn, are "seasonal," open only during the summer months. Dedman's Photo is still right where it had always been and it is owned operated by the (great?) granddaughter of one of Skagway's earliest settlers, Barbara Dedman Kalen (with whom Ann and I on our previous trip had spent nearly two hours talking about Skagway past and present).

Next door, the Golden North Hotel—owned by the Dedman-Kalen family—is still conspicuous and indeed considerably spruced up from my time.

Aside from these and a few others, to my growing dismay all the old stores have been replaced by little box-like shops whose only purpose for existing is to satisfy the tastes of passing tourists, on whose spending Skagway now wholly depends. We encounter the first of these, the Red Onion Saloon, near the beginning of our walk up Broadway. Not far away is another, the Christmas Store, which is followed by the Alaska Fur Gallery, Alaska Kids Store, Moe's Frontier Bar/Liquor Store, The Brass Pic, Inhofe Carvers Gallery, Little Switzerland, Klondike Coffee and Crepes, Arctic Furs, the Historic Skagway Inn, the Homestead Shop, Frontier Excursions, Alaska Made USA (also known as Arctic Ritz), the Alaska Shoppe, Hunter Art Studio, Broadway Cuts, Frontier Excursions, and more....

The Pullen House, where one of the town's most colorful characters once entertained guests, has vanished, replaced by the Pullen Creek RV Park.

If the entire array of shops were magically transported to some street along the East or West Coast of the United States where summer vacationers flock to shop for their trinkets, doodads, and mementos, anyone passing by these stores in their new location would find them indistinguishable from all the rest.

Most of these shops are operated by people who spend only their summers in Skagway. Come September they will flee back to the Lower Forty-Eight. The September exodus will slim the summer population of around seven hundred down to about three hundred, the only residents who will stay through the fall, winter, and spring.

❈

Our walk up Broadway leaves me depressed, irritated, even a bit angry. Is this just one more sign of a decline of authenticity in American town and cities, I peevishly ask myself, and maybe even among Americans in general?

That afternoon we take a tour of the other Skagway, the Skagway where the remaining permanent residents continue to live. To my surprise and pleasure, off Broadway is a Skagway pretty much as I had remembered it.

We begin with a brief visit to the Dahl Memorial Clinic. Though it too was built after Dad and Mother left Skagway, his service as a physician is recalled not only by its name but by a citation prominently displayed near its entrance. From there we head down to the first place we lived in after we arrived in Skagway, "the Tropea House" that had so cheerfully greeted us in January, 1926 with its display of bright pansies, still blooming in January. It has scarcely changed in appearance. The entrance on the small porch is exactly as I remember it. I see the dormers to the bedroom where Lew and I slept and the long shed, now a garage, where the cords of firewood were stored.

We move on nearer the Bay to "the Rapuzzi house," our second and last home in Skagway. It, too, looks pretty much unchanged. I'm snapping photos of the house from the middle of the street when a woman appears at the door. She waves to us, inviting us to come closer. In a friendly manner she asks why we're photographing the house. I explain.

At once she responds: "Dr. Dahl's son? Your dad delivered me." Her next words are: "Please come in." Which we do.

She is Phyllis Olson Brown, a treasure trove of information about the Skagway I had known. Her family connections to the old Skagway radiate in every direction. She is the daughter of Phil Olson whose mother died in giving him birth and who was adopted into the large Feero family, and whom I remember, though he was a half dozen years older than I, as one of Skagway's best athletes. Her mother Florence was one of Dad's nurses at the hospital. Her mother's sister, her aunt Edna, was George Rapuzzi's wife. It was from George that Phyllis had inherited the house in which we now stood.

She shows us through the house. Though it is changed in many ways, the splendid glassed-in porch that evokes so many memories is still there at the front of the house.

We speak of people I had known. Though most of them have died or left, a few, I learn, are living still in Skagway.

Memories that had faded over the years regain some of their vividness. I'm now glad, after all, that I have come to Skagway, one last time.

Standing on the porch I gaze out again on those magnificent mountains with their peaks and glaciers, their granite heights and wooded slopes, their lakes and streams and waterfalls.

I have no doubt that Skagway will change, perhaps in some ways not to my liking. But I fervently hope that this lovely piece of our world will be preserved as long as human beings, and our fellow creatures who inhabit those splendid mountains, valleys, forests, rivers, streams, and, yes, even the glaciers, continue to live on this earth.

Skagway, the Lynn Canal, and the Mountains Beyond

Photograph Credits

Personal Collection of the Author
Page 21: The Tropea House. Page 59: The Hospital. Page 78: The Rapuzzi House. Page 79: An Evening on the Front Porch. Page 107: Heading up the Tracks. Page 111: Lunch in the Sun. Page 118: Dreaming of Glory, Age 10 or 11. Page 125: Lew with a Goat, Myself with a Goat. Page 126: A Full Pack. Page 134: Lew with the Bear, Myself with the Bear. Page 135: The Mighty Hunters. Page 138: Mother and Dad. Page 158: Glacier Bay around 1933, Margery Glacier. Page 176: Best Wishes from Skagway.

Alaska State Library
P. O. Box 110571, Juneau, Alaska 99811
Page 9: Soapy Smith in His Saloon (Image 277-1-9)

Dedman's Photo Shop & Art Gallery
P. O. Box 317, Skagway, AK 99840
Cover: Skagway and Lynn Canal. Page 2: Skagway from the Sea. Page 50: Broadway. Page 90: The School. Page 114: The Basketball Team. Page 147: Martin Itjen.

Library of Congress, American Memory Collection
101 Independence Ave, SE, Washington, DC 20540
Page 105: White Pass Railroad Train 17 Miles from Skagway
(Reproduction Number LC-USZ62-120293)

Scott Mulvihill
P. O. Box 396, Skagway, AK 99840
Page 181: Skagway, the Lynn Canal, and the Mountains Beyond.

University of Alaska
907 Yukon Drive, Fairbanks, AK 99775
Page 8: Harriet Pullen ("Threads of Gold—Women of the Alaska Gold Rush" Collection.)

Washington Libraries, Special Collections Division
Seattle, WA 98195
Page 5: Dyea Wharf, Circa 1897. (Neg. # Hegg58). Page 6: Chilkoot Pass, Winter of 1898 (Neg. # Hegg97). Page 7: White Pass, Winter of 1899 (Neg. # Hegg124); Page 162: Tlingit Carved Wood Figures (Neg. # NA2556). Page 163: Three brothers, headmen of the Chilkat Tlingit, Alaska, 1907 (Neg. # SHS 11,398).

About the Author

After graduating from the University in Washington in 1936, Robert Dahl entered the Department of Government of Yale University. He spent the academic year 1937-38 in Washington, D.C., as an intern at the National Labor Relations Board, where he met a fellow intern, Mary Louise Bartlett. In 1940, he received his Ph.D. from Yale in 1940, married Mary (they would have four children), and moved to Washington, where he worked in the Department of Agriculture, the Office of Price Administration, and the War Production Board.

In March 1943 he entered the U.S. Army and was assigned as a private to a regimental intelligence and reconnaissance platoon in the 44th Infantry Division, where he served until after V E Day in May, 1945. Having risen to the rank of platoon sergeant, in France he received a battlefield commission as a second lieutenant.

After returning to the United States at the end of 1945, he gained an appointment to the Department of Government at Yale University, where he remained until his retirement at the age of 70 in 1986.

As author, co-author, or editor he has published twenty-three books and a hundred articles, many written after his retirement, mainly dealing with various aspects of democratic theory and practice. In 1995, Who Governs? (1961) was listed by the London Times Literary Supplement as one of "the hundred most influential books since the war." On Democracy, published in 1998, has been translated into more than twenty languages.

His wife Mary died in 1970, and in 1973 he married Ann Sale Barber and became the stepfather of two daughters. He and his wife Ann have continued to live in Connecticut.

Printed in the United States
120247LV00001B/56/A